as one with Authority

as one with Authority

by
John R. Brokhoff

BRISTOL BOOKS
WILMORE, KY 40390

AS ONE WITH AUTHORITY
The Ministry of Preaching

© 1989 by John R. Brokhoff
Published by Bristol Books

First Edition, July 1989

All rights reserved. Except for brief quotations embodied in critical articles and reviews, no part of this book may be used or reproduced in any manner without written permission.

Unless otherwise indicated all Scripture quotations are from the *Holy Bible*, the New International Version. © 1973, 1978, 1984 by the International Bible Society. Used by permission.

Scripture quotations indicated (RSV) are from the Revised Standard Bible. © 1946, 1952, 1971 by the Division of Christian Education of the National Council of the Church of Christ in the U.S.A. Used by permission.

Scripture quotations indicated (KJV) are from the King James Bible.

Library of Congress Number: 89-60626
ISBN: 0-917851-35-8
Suggested Subject Headings:
1. Preaching
Recommended Dewey Decimal Classification: 251

BRISTOL BOOKS
An imprint of the Forum for Scriptural Christianity, Inc.
308 East Main Street • Wilmore, Kentucky 40390

Contents

Dedicated to
Bishop William R. Cannon
and
Dr. G. Ray Jordan
Who gave me the opportunity
to teach Homiletics at Candler School of Theology
Emory University
Altanta, Georgia
1950-55, 1965-80

Foreword

Philip Brooks, in the Lyman Beecher Lectureship on Preaching, which is a series of lectures he gave during the first decade after the lectureship was founded at Yale in 1871, defined preaching "as the bringing of truth through personality." Fred B. Craddock, a more recent lecturer on that same lectureship and the Bandy Professor of Preaching on the faculty of the Candler School of Theology of Emory University, says that preaching is too complex and difficult a subject to be defined. He prefers to label it an activity consisting of many variables such as the message, the messenger, the recipients, the method of preparation, the manner of delivery and perhaps still others.

Though Brooks bases his discussion of preaching on a clear-cut definition and Craddock bases his on an activity in the process of being performed, their results are more remarkably the same. Craddock insists that the personality of the preacher is vital in the effectiveness of his or her work from the pulpit, for he believes that the sermon is invariably a self-disclosure of the person of faith, passion, authority and grace. Brooks affirms that the two basic elements in effective preaching are the personality of the preacher and the truth of his or her message. Brooks insists that truth without a convincing personality to communicate it is not preached truth. But a convincing and compelling personality who advances his own opinions rather than the truth of God cannot qualify as a preacher.

Both Brooks and Craddock take into account the nature of the congregation in the success of preaching. Brooks, in the more traditional way, interprets the role of the congregation passively—namely, as a body of people with needs that the sermon is designed to meet. The preacher must be sensitive enough to discern those needs and to speak poignantly to them to express the truth of

God in satisfying them. He abhors cleverness, sarcasm and any form of sensationalism used to attract attention and entertain the congregation. Craddock assigns the congregation a positive role in preaching. He says a sermon must move in such a way that people in the pews actually think along with the preacher as he or she speaks and feel the same emotions the preacher feels. In other words, the listeners must not think they are being spoken to but that they are a part of the act of preaching itself. Both Philip Brooks and Fred Craddock are people-oriented in their preaching.

The approach of John R. Brokhoff in this book, *As One With Authority,* is altogether theocentric in outlook and application. He thinks of the preacher as a prophet, as one called out and set apart, as God's person proclaiming God's message and entirely at God's disposal to do what God wants done. "When people come to church," he writes, "they come not to hear a human but God. They want to know who God is, where he can be found and what his will is for their lives." If preaching is primarily an art, then it stands alongside music, the liturgy, Christian symbols, inspirational stories and other art forms conducive to public and private worship. It is just one among many of the means of grace. Brokhoff insists that preaching is much more than just one of the means of grace. For Protestants it is *the* means of grace. "If it is true that preaching is God speaking, then we can see at once that there is nothing more important in the life and work of the church than preaching. Is anybody's voice more needed than God's?" The sole text of preaching is whether or not the sermon saves souls. "It brings people to Christ. Lives are changed through good preaching. It is the church's chief source of power."

To Brokhoff there is in reality only one sacrament, and that sacrament is the Word. Baptism and the Lord's Supper give visibility to the Word, while preaching is the Word's oral expression. "In preaching, the Word not only speaks but acts."

Both Brokhoff and Craddock are biblical preachers, and both emphasize the importance of using the lectionary for the scriptural passages on which to build the sermon. Dr. G. Ray Jordan, Dr. Brokhoff's predecessor in the chair of preaching at Emory, was neither. He was almost altogether a topical preacher who chose his subject for the sermon and then sought a biblical text to support it. I doubt that he ever looked at a lectionary. But, like Brokhoff and Craddock, Jordan was a very gifted and powerful preacher. He stood in the tradition of Harry Emerson Fosdick.

Brokhoff and Craddock are more alike than they are different. Both base every word and thought in the sermon on the Word of God. But their approaches are different. Craddock always has in mind the listening congregation, its needs and longings, so that in a very real sense it actually helps him frame his message. Brokhoff, in contrast, feels he as the preacher has a message from the Lord, and, like Jeremiah, that message burns within him until he gives it utterance in the face of a congregation. Craddock makes the sermon synonymous with persuasion, so he employs humor and gentle coaxing. Brokhoff sees the sermon as proclamation. Craddock tells the gospel story, which people still long to hear as in days long ago, though he tells it in a contemporary setting. Brokhoff expounds the Scripture and then applies its principles to people's lives.

I am persuaded we need both. Craddock dominates the homiletical scene today. He is without a rival as a teacher of preaching. His book entitled *Preaching* is the standard text. Brokhoff's *As One With Authority* is a wholesome addition to the homiletical field. Comparable in style and thought to Craddock's book, it will complement his work and add an entirely new dimension to contemporary preaching. With Craddock, preaching takes us to the Word. With Brokhoff, preaching brings the Word to us.

I was Dean of Candler School of Theology of Emory University when John Brokhoff joined our faculty. I am proud to commend his book to the reading public.

William R. Cannon,
Bishop of the United Methodist Church and
Honorary President of the World Methodist Council.

Introduction

In 1974 Fred Craddock, my successor as professor of preaching at Emory's Candler School of Theology, published his *As One Without Authority*. It marked the watershed in twentieth-century preaching. There was a transition from deductive to inductive preaching.

This change can be seen in books by a father and son, for example. In the first half of this century George Buttrick's *Jesus Came Preaching* expressed the style of preaching for his generation. His son, David, recently published his *Homiletic*, which describes preaching for the second half of the century.

The title of Fred Craddock's book, *As One Without Authority*, at first appears misleading. On first impression one gathers that a preacher has no authority. However, the book deals not with the authority of content but with the method of preaching. We are to have authority in content but not authoritarianism in delivery or approach.

The World Has Changed

Since the sixties the world has rapidly changed. People now resent authoritarian presentations. Like Soviet Premier Mikhail Gorbachev's comment in 1988 that he was tired of U.S. President Ronald Reagan's sermons, today the slogan is "Don't preach to me." Today people do not want to be told what to think, believe or do. They want to do their own thinking and come to their own conclusions about the truth. They want to ask questions and discuss issues.

The former monological, authoritarian method no longer is effective. The old method was dogmatic and dictatorial. Preachers either said, or implied, "Keep quiet and listen!" or "This is the truth—accept it" or "Believe it or else" or "It is for you to do and die and not to question why." The congregation was to be passive and courteous in paying attention while the preacher orated from his high pulpit. But the new style of preaching is inductive, dialogical and conversational; and it involves the congregation in a two-way mode of communication. The book *As One Without Authority* pioneered this new direction.

The problem in preaching today is that we have gone to the other extreme. We have become non-authoritarian in our method and style, but we also have denied authority in the content of preaching.

According to Scripture, a preacher is to speak with authority without being authoritarian. Jesus is our example. He had authority in what he said, but he did not say it as an authoritarian. "He taught as one who had authority, and not as their teachers of the law" (Matthew 7:29).

The elders and chief priests (the authorities of the day) asked Christ, "By what authority are you doing these things?" (Matthew 21:23). Jesus prefaced his great commission: "All authority in heaven and on earth has been given to me" (Matthew 28:18).

Jesus spoke with authority—"But I say to you." With authority he exorcised demons and healed the sick (Mark 1:27). But at the same time he was not authoritarian in his method. He asked questions such as, "What do you think?" "How do you read?" "Who was neighbor to the stricken man?" or "Do you believe in the Son of man?" In preaching he invited the people's thought: "Consider the lilies of the field." and "Come, let us reason together" expressed his non-authoritarian style. The challenge a preacher faces today is to have an authoritative message without an authoritarian attitude, approach or method. Is it possible to proclaim an authoritative truth without becoming authoritarian?

As One Without Authority

We are not here speaking of authority as applied to the method of presentation of the preached Word, but rather of the content of what is preached. Serious consequences result from today's lack of authority in the message we preach. Consider some of them.

There is the consequence, first, of not meeting the spiritual needs of our people. In the last decade or two, mainline Protestant churches in America have lost members by the millions. Where are these people going? Into the world of total unbelief? No, studies show that seventy-eight percent of them are joining conservative and fundamentalist churches where they are getting messages of strong authority. People are hungry for something definite and positive. They want to know what is safe to believe and what is the right way to live. If the mainline churches want to stop declining and start growing again, they need to proclaim messages of authority.

Another consequence of preaching as one without authority is topical preaching. This type of preaching is humanistic. It is preacher-centered. The preacher chooses a topic or subject and gives his personal opinions about the solution. These opinions are usually illustrated by personal experiences. In a recently published sermon, seventy-seven references to the preacher were found. There is no authority in this kind of preaching except the authority of the preacher and his or her experiences.

A preacher is a human with limited wisdom and understanding. One cannot base a faith on what a human says or believes. Consequently, a topical preacher repeatedly says "I think" or "I submit" or "I suggest," etc. The solution is biblical preaching where the truth of the sermon comes directly from the text, where the sermon is not the preacher's wisdom but God's revealed truth. It is not what the preacher says but "thus saith the Lord."

Third, if the preacher is one without authority in his or her message, he or she has only questions and no answers. A weakness of today's pulpit is that it asks only questions and gives no answers.

But people want answers. They already have their questions. If the preacher raises a question, there must be an authoritative answer. If we do not have a solution, we offer a stone instead of bread. Suppose Jesus had no answer to the question, "What must I do to inherit eternal life?" Or, suppose Paul had no answer to the Philippian jailer's question, "What must I do to be saved?" Or, what would the people at Pentecost have done if Peter had given no answer to their question, "What then must we do?"

As a preacher, do you have an answer to these basic questions: "Is God real?" "Is Jesus the Son of God?" "Is there life after death?" What is faith?" "Am I a person of worth?" What a crime if you have no answer!

How you give the answer is another problem. It is to be given in a non-authoritarian way. We are to lead and help people to find the God-given answer for themselves.

A fourth consequence of preaching without a message of authority is that the preacher has no message of deep conviction. This is not what people want or need. They want a sure word, something simple, direct and plain. One without authority in his or her message says, "If you do not all repent, after a fashion, and confess your sins, so to speak, you will all be damned, as it were."

William Willimon tells of a woman who asked a certain pastor, "What does the church believe about pre-marital sex?" He replied, "What do *you* think about pre-marital sex?" She protested, "I know that pastors don't approve." He said, "*Some* pastors, older pastors." She continued, "Isn't the Bible against people just living together?" He answered, "The Bible is a culturally-conditioned book that must be read with interpretative sophistication. The main thing is to be sure you're open, trusting, loving and caring." People deserve more certainty than that.

Consider a fifth consequence of preaching as one without authority. If one has no message of authority the sermon cannot be presented with conviction, confidence or urgency. Persuasive preaching is based upon convictions that the message is true and vital. It is a matter of life and death. If there is no authority, the sermon is presented without zeal or concern for acceptance by the listeners. A preacher can say with authority, "This is the truth. Here is life. Here is peace with God. Here is salvation."

This conviction affects the delivery of the sermon. The message demands urgency, zeal, passion and enthusiasm; thus the preacher speaks with dignity. He or she speaks as an ambassador of the King and by his authority. There is no hemming or hawing or hesitation.

What we are saying is that a preacher should have a message of authority but express it in a non-authoritarian way. But the question remains, "Where does a preacher get this authority?" Jesus was asked the same question by the religious leaders of his day. "By what authority are you doing these things? . . . And who gave you this authority?" (Matthew 21:23).

God the Father is the ultimate and only Source of all authority, because God is God and there is no Other nor any greater. In Romans 13:1 Paul affirms this. "There is no authority except that which God has established." Any authority anyone else has received came as a gift. Jesus said that his authority came from the Father. "And he has given him authority to judge because he is the Son of Man" (John 5:27).

And Jesus passed on authority to the disciples and "called the Twelve together, he gave them power and authority . . ." (Luke 9:1). This authority is passed down to today's disciples.

Authority from God

A preacher, then, has authority given by God himself. A true preacher has been called by God to preach, just as Abraham, Moses and the prophets were called to speak for God and to serve him. The call of God is the basic foundation of a preacher's life and work. Preaching is based on a divine directive to be God's spokesperson.

The authority to preach and the content of our preaching comes from God through Christ, for Christ is the Son of God, "God of God, Light of light, very God of very God" (Nicene Creed). When we preach Christ we are given the authority to speak for him and to continue his ministry. His name is the authority to heal. He has given us the authority to forgive sins in his name. In the liturgy of the church a pastor pronounces absolution. "As a called and ordained pastor of the Church of Christ, and by his authority, I therefore declare to you the entire forgiveness of all your sins."

The authority of God comes to us in and through God's Word. The Holy Scriptures are a record of God's self-revelation. It is a book of God by God. Thus it is a book of truth and life. The truth is of God and is therefore authoritative in matters of faith and life. Thus, preaching from the Bible is authoritative preaching. The authority comes not from the personality or opinions of the preacher but from the biblical truth that is proclaimed. Preaching, then, is the Word of God and has inherent authority.

God's authority comes to the preacher also through the church. What is the church? It is the body of Christ. The treasure of the church is the Word and the sacraments. At ordination the church gives authority to proclaim the Word. With the laying on of hands, a bishop says to an ordinand, "Take thou authority to preach the Word and to administer the holy sacraments in the church." Now the ordinand speaks with the authority of the Word and the church. He or she now represents the church and speaks for it as well as for God. The teachings of the church are authoritative so long as they are in conformity with the Scriptures.

In the light of all this how can anyone claim that a preacher is one who speaks without authority? The preacher has the authority of God, Christ, the Scriptures, the truth and the church. With this authority he or she can proclaim the good news of the gospel with confidence, conviction and boldness. And yet how tragic that in order to get a hearing in our modern world, a preacher thinks he or she must give the message of authority as one who is without authority.

Part I

The Milieu of Preaching

The standard of preaching in the modern world is deplorable. There are few great preachers. Many clergy do not seem to believe in it anymore as a powerful way in which to proclaim the gospel and change the life. This is the age of the sermonette, and sermonettes make Christianettes.

—John R. W. Stott

* * * * *

The church must be divine, else it would never have survived such preaching.

—Reinhold Niebuhr

Chapter 1

The Challenge of Preaching Today

How can a preacher be heard in today's world? Is it possible to get people to listen to and accept the preached Word? We live in a world that says, "Don't preach to me."

A parish pastor preaching Sunday after Sunday may face various distractions and handicaps that make it hard to get a message across. Crying babies and noisy children compete with the sermon. Whispering teenagers usually on the last pew or in the balcony disturb a preacher's concentration. I shall never forget the boy on the front pew directly in front of the pulpit mimicking me with his mouth and hands while I was preaching! There are loud noises of trucks, airplanes, trains or power saws that drown out portions of the sermon. Occasionally a person comes in late or leaves early during the sermon and all eyes go to the moving person.

These are only minor and superficial distractions. There are much larger obstacles to overcome such as the reluctance to hear the message. The problem is how to get people to listen to the Word. Jesus faced this problem (Luke 7:31-35). He compared people to children. When wedding music was played, they would not dance. When funeral songs were sung, they would not cry. He complained that they would not listen to him nor to John the Baptizer.

The prophets had the same problem. They were so desperate to get God's message across that they tried almost anything. For three years Isaiah went naked to communicate that Assyria would lead those who trusted in Egypt, naked into captivity (Isaiah 20:1-3). Jeremiah went around wearing a wooden yoke to tell the people that God wanted them to bear the yoke of Babylonia (Jeremiah 27:1-3). In great fervor he cried, "O land, land, land, hear the word of the Lord!" (Jeremiah 22:29). When Ezekiel's wife died, God ordered him not to mourn for her to teach the nation not to mourn at the coming destruction of Jerusalem (Ezekiel 24:15-21). To demonstrate God's love for a faithless people, Hosea took back his Gomer who had committed adultery (Hosea 3:1).

Probably each generation feels it is the most difficult to get a hearing for the gospel, but it seems harder to get that hearing today than at any other period of history. Why is this so? And can this claim be substantiated?

The Impact of the Media

What has the greatest influence on American society? The Bible? The church? Preachers? No, it is the media—television, radio and press. Today most people live by the media rather than by the Bible. It has taken the place of the church in telling people how to behave, what to believe, what to value and what to regard as meaningful. How can a preacher successfully compete with the media? It seems hopeless and frustrating.

The media has great influence on society because it reaches far more people than does the pulpit. In the United States there are 1,169 television stations, 9000 radio outlets and 1,759 daily newspapers. Ninety-nine percent of American homes own at least one television set. Sixty-five percent own a VCR.

Moreover, the media attracts more of people's time than the pulpit does. Americans watch television on an average of seven hours daily. At age seventy, a person will have spent eight years watching television. By the time of high school graduation, a student spends more time in front of the television set than in the classroom.

What is the media proclaiming? What messages are coming across? These are just a few:

• The fittest survive. Violence is glorified.

• Happiness consists of the abundance of possessions. This encourages greed and living beyond one's income. Consequently, Americans owe three trillion dollars in foreign and domestic obligations, resulting in America being the world's largest debtor nation with a forty billion dollar debt.

• Consumption of goods is inherently good. To encourage consumption, the media uses commercials. By the time of graduation from high school, a student sees 350,000 commercials.

• Property and power are more important than people. Human values are subordinated to property values. Consequently, the natural order is destroyed by commercial investment and development.

• Progress is inevitable and inherently good regardless of the cost.

The problem is: How can a preacher, in twenty minutes once a week, counteract the daily and continuous bombardment of these unchristian values?

Secular Humanism

To a large extent modern society lives according to secular humanism. It is an ideology that consists of non-Christian myths. The focus is upon the human being as the highest value of life. The human is put in the place of God. Secular humanism promotes the following myths:

• One's environment gives meaning to life.

• Immortality consists of one's continued influence in the world.

• Narcissism: The person is the end-all of life. One deserves only the best. The proud, self-centered humanist says, "I owe it to myself to spend all my money on myself."

- What is right and wrong? "We'll take a vote and decide." Morals are relative.
- What is new is good; the old is bad.
- Whatever makes you feel good is good.
- Who is God that we should be mindful of him?

The question is, How can one preach in the face of these generally held anti-Christian views? These secular views challenge the preacher to persuade people to change their views to those taught in the Bible. The need of our day is for persuasive preaching.

The World's Lifestyle

How can one get a hearing for righteousness in a world that embraces sin? Sinful ways have become a normal, accepted lifestyle in today's society. The common response of those indicted with crimes is, "I have done nothing wrong." Their slogan is, "Everybody's doing it!" Sinful living has become so normal that few are embarrassed or shocked at sins previously considered shameful. We Americans have become a people who no longer know how to blush.

It is a paradox of our times that we are a sin-saturated society with the least consciousness of sin. We are marinated in sin so that every level and area of society are penetrated. *Time* magazine (February 22, 1988) reports,

> A moral alarm clock is going off in America. Children are growing up in an atmosphere abuzz with libidinous solicitings, sitting transfixed before Technicolor celebrations of greed and lust and violence, lured through many conduits toward experiment with drugs or rebellion. Authority is undermined as parents drift apart or desert the home, to be replaced by teachers who are morally adrift. . . . Pornography is available on home screens by cable television or VCRs. Divorce, living together without marriage and homosexuality are common.

Many of these people are in our congregations. Since one out of every two marriages is failing, many divorced people and single parents are part of worshiping congregations. Since twenty-two percent of all births in America are illegitimate, we have unwed mothers and illegitimate children in our churches. We have youth who are indulging in premarital sex, for fifty percent of all youth have sex before graduating from high school and sixty-five percent of church youth have sex by age eighteen. In America more than two million couples are living together without benefit of marriage. Some of these couples may be in church Sunday mornings.

In addition to this sexual collapse, we face family disintegration, governmental corruption, scandal, drug addiction and even some television evangelists' moral failures.

How shall we preach to these people? Of course, if there is true repentance and amendment of life, there is the message of comfort from divine forgiveness and acceptance. To a sinful people the Word cries out, "Repent and believe the gospel." But the world does not buy this. With the sexual crisis we are urged to participate in "safe sex" by using condoms and thus prevent AIDS and unwanted pregnancies. For sexually active youth, sex education in schools teaches them how to use contraceptives. When something gets out of hand and we are no longer able to control its spread, we resort to legalization.

Yet, in spite of this avalanche of sin, many preach only about the love and grace of God. We are strangely mum when it comes to proclaiming the law of God. Since the Word consists of law and gospel, we are proclaiming only half of the Word if we confine our preaching to the gospel. Today's sin-saturated society calls for the preaching of the law to bring us to repentance.

Preaching During a Storm

When we preach we want quiet, peace and order. Can you imagine yourself preaching during a storm? Today's society is in no ordinary storm; it is in a hurricane. Winds blow at one hundred miles per hour. Trees are falling.

Homes are crushed. People are hurt and dying. Life is full of confusion and trauma.

The wild winds of secularism, materialism, hedonism and humanism are turning the world upside down. Everything good that has been nailed down has come loose and is flying around. Morally and spiritually we are in an uproar. How can one preach in the midst of this chaos?

No past generation has had to face as many radical changes as that of the past fifty years. We have lived through a social revolution involving civil rights. Our youth have rebelled against authority expressed in rock music, sex and drugs. In the past fifty years we have lived through three wars which brought physical handicaps and death to millions. In transportation we have gone from the Model-T Ford to supersonic jets that fly faster than the speed of sound. We have even put men on the moon. We have gone from an industrial to a technological age with radio, television, VCRs and computers. We have gone from dynamite to nuclear fission that has given us bombs capable of killing a million people on the first attack.

These radical changes have made us insecure and fearful. We are worried about the future. We sense we are living on the precipice of doom. We are faced with speed without direction, power without control. We have strong means but weak ends. We remember the words of General Omar Bradley in a 1948 Armistice Day address:

> We have too many men of science, too few men of God. We have grasped the mystery of the atom, and rejected the Sermon on the Mount. Ours is a world of nuclear giants and ethical infants. We know more about war than about peace, more about killing than we know about living.

In this uproar and turmoil, how can we get a hearing for the gospel? The voice of the preacher must be loud enough for people to hear him or her above the noise. Perhaps we need to speak like God in the time of Amos:

"The Lord *roars* from Zion and *thunders* from Jerusalem"
(Amos 1:2, italics mine).

Contented Church People

Most of us preach to church people. We are not on
radio or television speaking to the world, even if the world
would listen. We are not on the street corners proclaiming
the gospel. We preach inside churches where God's
people have gathered to worship and to hear the Word.
Do these church people make it easy to preach because
of their eagerness and receptivity to the Word? In many
cases contented church people challenge the preacher to
get across God's message to them. Many a preacher
would say with Jesus, "He who has ears to hear, let him
hear." His parable of the sower deals with the problem of
hearing the Word, and only one-fourth of the soil received
it fruitfully. Would that be a correct proportion of our
church people?

Why do church people constitute a challenge to
preaching? For one thing, many churches consist of the
self-satisfied and contented. They are, on the whole, nice,
respectable and "good" people. They sense no need to
change or to be converted. Probably our preaching in the
past is to blame for this condition. We keep telling them
they are the people of God, the saved society, the fellowship of the redeemed. We repeat that God loves each one
and values each one. They get the feeling they "have it
made." They are lulled to sleep by the messages of "cheap
grace."

Secondly, it is difficult to preach to a modern congregation because the people are knowledgeable about
biblical stories and church teachings. They have been
sitting in their accustomed pews for years and years. They
are callous from hearing sermons Sunday after Sunday,
year after year. They know the gospel. They have heard
the Christmas and Easter accounts. They have heard
sermons repeatedly on the same lections. So, what is
new? The preacher asks, "What can I say that I have not
already said?" For this reason preaching on Christmas,

Easter and Pentecost is the most difficult. With indifferent eyes the congregation looks to the pulpit as if to say, "Same old song, same verse." Many of our faithful have become dull of hearing. For some, listening to a sermon is like doing penance.

A third reason that makes preaching to church people a challenge is that many are affluent. Our churches are largely composed of middle and upper classes. You will not find the homeless, the street people nor the folks on the other side of the track in church. If they did come, they would probably make the regular attenders uncomfortable. Because of their affluence, many church members have a false security. They trust in their education, professional skills, good jobs, high salaries, financial investments, unions, corporations or fringe benefits— their Dow Jones average of success. For some, their goal is an early and comfortable retirement. The result can be indifference to the call of Christ. As Peter Marshall once said, "Indifferent people cannot build a different world."

Meeting the Challenge

At no time in Christian history has a preacher faced a greater challenge to proclaim the gospel. It seems as though everything is against the acceptance of the Word in a secular world which considers religion to be obsolete. How can the average preacher meet this challenge?

First, confront the challenge with courage. It is like a mountain climber challenged to climb the highest mountain. Or it is like setting out to reach the South Pole. It is facing a monster or a giant as David faced Goliath. The challenge is in the challenge. It is a challenge to do the "impossible." In the words of Maltby Babcock:

> We are not here to drift, to dream, to play.
> We have hard work to do and loads to lift.
> Shun not the struggle. Face it.
> 'Tis God's gift.

Second, fight the battle with proper equipment. David could not use Saul's armor to fight Goliath. He had to use his own armor—stones and a slingshot. As preachers we need to know the world and people's questions, needs and problems. We must speak their language so they will understand us. We must fight fire with fire. If we are going to get a hearing, we will have to adapt our methods. For instance, one-, two- or three-hour sermons of the past will not go over in a "fast food society." Research reveals that the average congregation has an interest span of only five to seven minutes. This calls for a method of recreating interest every seven minutes. Again, the method of communication has changed from monological to dialogical style. The former authoritarian, deductive style is not as effective as a quiet, conversational method of preaching. It is not, "I speak; you listen," but rather, "Come, let us reason together."

Third, learn to be creative. "New" is the magic word in selling products. People are ever interested in something new. It is the same in preaching. Take a new approach to an old problem. Try a new way of constructing the sermon. Have a startling introduction. Close the sermon with a bang. Wake up the congregation. Make them think by giving the old wine of the gospel in new wineskins. This calls for study, meditation and solitude. Carl Sandburg said that Shakespeare, Leonardo da Vinci, Franklin and Lincoln did not have movies but loneliness which put them in a creative mood.

Fourth, draw upon spiritual resources. No person can preach on his or her own power. But fortunately a preacher has tremendous spiritual resources; prayer, the Holy Spirit and faith. It takes divine help to go on preaching when you feel that preaching is foolishness. Often we preach on and on and see no results. Then we draw upon our trust that God's Word will accomplish its purpose. We take courage to prepare next Sunday's sermon.

Fifth, be content to be faithful, not successful. As St. Paul wrote, we are to be faithful stewards of the divine mysteries. Who is a successful preacher? Who can say what "success" is? Only God knows. Our homiletical task is to be faithful in doing our best to proclaim the Word.

Has Preaching a Place in Church Growth?

Where does preaching fit into the current emphasis on church growth? If it has a place, is it in first or last place of importance? Or perhaps it has no place at all.

Consider the facts. A director of evangelism recently wrote in a church periodical that we are a *dying* church. One denomination is losing members at the rate of a thousand members per week. Another denomination reports a decrease of twenty-five percent over the past ten years. Almost every mainline Protestant church in America is aboard the sinking ship "Church." Are we alarmed at this sad state of affairs?

Another fact is equally disturbing. In America we have a great potential for numerical growth. Ninety-six million (forty percent) are unchurched and seventy-five million (thirty-one percent) are inactive members, making a total of 171 million potential church members! The truth is that the numbers are declining when the harvest of souls is plenteous.

What can be done about this annual decline and great potential growth? Does preaching have anything to do with it? Recently a pastor wrote an article offering a fourfold solution for each congregation, but preaching was not listed as one of the ways to gain growth. Apparently for him preaching has nothing to do with church growth.

When we consider the down-playing of preaching during the past twenty-five years, we need not be surprised. During this time we put emphasis on worship with new service books and hymnals. We learned to chant the liturgy, wear chasubles and celebrate communion weekly. But all of this did not stop the membership decline. We turned to counseling as a more effective method than preaching, but it did not produce growth. Many pastors focused on small groups rather than mass preaching, but in many cases all this approach amounted to was shared ignorance. In seminaries students were urged to "get in touch with yourselves" when we should have taught "get in touch with God." We put our trust in mergers, but they resulted in an actual loss of members.

Try the Best

We have tried all of the above methods and none has stopped the decline. We have tried the rest; now is the time to try the best—preaching! It is not the only method of church growth, but it is the very best!

What, you ask, does preaching have to do with church growth? You say that unchurched people are not in church today to hear preaching. Or, you may say, modern people do not want to be preached to. How then can preaching gain members?

To answer the question of preaching's relationship to church growth, we must first look at the primary task of a minister. In 1745 the Wesleys and their nine preachers adopted the following rules: "You have nothing to do but to save souls; therefore, spend and be spent in this work."

If the primary task of a minister is to save souls, what is his or her chief means of saving souls? Is it preaching? P.T. Forsyth wrote, "Preaching is the most distinctive institution in Christianity. With its preaching Christianity rises or falls." Similarly Luther claimed, "There is only one obligation, that of preaching." If Christianity depends on preaching, then the current sad state of preaching explains why the church is not growing.

You may ask, How does good preaching produce growth? People come into the church through attendance at worship services. Good preaching draws visitors and brings out the members. If the preaching is good, the people return next Sunday and the next for more of the gospel. Attendance is usually a good barometer of the quality of preaching. Empty pews should make a preacher ask, "What is wrong with my preaching? Why aren't my sermons attracting more people?"

Moreover, preaching motivates members to witness. They are inspired, helped and fed. They become excited and enthusiastic about the church. They boast of their preacher and tell others to come and hear him or her. Of course, the unchurched are not in church on a Sunday morning. They must be reached and brought to church. A recent study revealed that a church member knows an average of eight unchurched people. If a church has one hundred members, it has eight hundred potential members. Good preaching will motivate members to bring their unchurched friends to worship.

Good preaching also attracts visitors who become prospects for membership. Visitors keep coming; they eventually accept Christ and join the church. People are not serious prospects until they start attending services. Growing churches make contact with these visitors before the next Sunday, and one pastor telephones each visitor the same Sunday afternoon.

Therefore, all preaching needs to be evangelistic (though not evangelistic in terms of emotionalism, sentimentalism, manipulation, hell, fire and brimstone or undue pressure from the pulpit). Regardless of the type of sermon—inductive, doctrinal, narrative, dialogue, life-situation—the ultimate end is to bring people to faith or to a greater faith in Christ. When we speak of evangelism, we mean full-orbed evangelism: making Christians (come to Christ), maturing Christians (come closer to Christ), re-making Christians (come back to Christ).

Evangelical Preaching

As a method of evangelism there is nothing wrong with preaching. The problem is the quality of preaching. It is not the average type of preaching that wins. It must be *good* preaching. But what is good preaching?

The first characteristic of good preaching is that it is evangelical. This means it must be biblical, for the "evangel" is the gospel of the Word Incarnate, and the Word is recorded in Scripture.

Preaching today is not what it should be because a biblical sermon in mainline churches is a rarity. In many cases a text is not announced, and if it is announced, it is ignored or used as a decoration for the sermon.

Biblical preaching attracts people to church because the power of preaching is in the Word and not in the person delivering the Word. Through Isaiah, Yahweh promises, "So is my word that goes out from my mouth: It will not return to me empty" (Isaiah 55:11).

People come to church to hear the Word of God. They are not interested in the preacher's opinions. They want to know what God's will is in today's predicament and to hear about God's grace for sinners.

When we built Redeemer Church in Atlanta, we had carved on the front of the pulpit the cry of Jeremiah, "O earth, earth, earth, hear the word of the Lord." To preach the Word of the Lord is to preach on a text from the Bible. Like a blooming flower that opens its petals to the sun, a preacher takes a text and lets it unfold with authority and certainty. People recognize it as coming from God and respond, "You'd better believe it!" or "You'd better do it!"

A second characteristic of evangelical preaching is that it is Christ-centered. Like the ancient Greeks, people are still looking to the pulpit and saying, "Sir, we wish to see Jesus."

When was the last time you heard or preached a sermon on Jesus? Some time ago Marcus Borg, associate professor of religious studies at Oregon State University, began an article in *Christian Century*: "I hear very few sermons about Jesus. True, sometimes a parable or saying or healing of Jesus may be preached on, but I seldom hear a sermon about Jesus."

Preaching about Jesus is what made Paul's preaching effective and productive. Under his preaching congregations were born. He said, "For we do not preach ourselves, but Jesus Christ as Lord" (2 Corinthians 4:5). When we finish a sermon the people should not say, "What a great preacher" but "What a great Christ!"

How can the preaching of Jesus bring people into the church? By proclaiming Jesus we are presenting the best, the finest, the most attractive human who ever lived, who lives now or who will ever live. His personality is irresistible. There is no one like him. There is something in the face of Jesus that makes us call him "Master." When he says, "Follow me," who dares to say "No"? Who can withstand his understanding, compassion, wisdom and appeal?

A third characteristic of evangelical preaching which causes church growth is the preaching of the cross. To preach Jesus is not enough, for one can preach him as a human, teacher, leader or wonder worker. In this case he is only a man. The significance of Jesus is that he is the Savior of the world by means of the cross. Because humanity's greatest need is reconciliation with God, the cross is desperately needed.

C.S. Lewis said, "Christianity has no message for those who do not realize that they are sinners." Because of the cross there is forgiveness. When theologian Karl Barth visited Union Seminary in New York, a group of professors met with him for a colloquy. One asked him, "If you were to meet Adolf Hitler, what would you say to him?" Quietly and simply he replied, "I would say to him, Jesus Christ died for your sins." In every sermon, therefore, the cross needs to be preached so that every person will get the answer to the question, "What must I do to be saved?"

How does preaching the cross attract new members? Today people are burdened with guilt. They will come to hear the gospel with the good news of forgiveness and deliverance. Moreover, there is the magnetism of the cross, for Jesus said, "But I, when I am lifted up from the earth, will draw all men to myself" (John 12:32). There is something about the suffering, the tears, the agony and the sacrifice of one dying on our behalf that draws us to believe in him. Isn't this expressed in some of our hymns? "When I survey the wondrous cross. . . . Love so amazing, so divine, demands my soul, my life, my all."

Passionate Preaching

In one church the preaching was so uninteresting that a sign was put on the inside of the pulpit quoting Hebrews 11:4 (KJV)—"He being dead yet speaketh." So often a preacher speaks without unction, zeal, life or enthusiasm. It sounds as though he or she could not care less about the subject matter. Often there is no fire in the pulpit. Elton Trueblood once defined the church as the "incendiary fellowship." Maybe it would be more correct to call it a "cinder fellowship." As a guest preacher I get into quite a few pulpits. It is interesting to see what is kept in pulpits: electronic equipment, hymnals, past church bulletins and a potpourri of discards. Now and then I find in a pulpit a fire extinguisher as though flames might break out in the pulpit. But to this date I have never seen in a pulpit a fire extinguisher that was used! If the pulpit is not on fire, the pews will never catch fire with the gospel.

People will not come nor join the church if the sermon bores them to tears. A sermon needs to be alive and fervent. The preacher needs to be zealous, excited and enthusiastic about his or her message. Abraham Lincoln once said, "When I hear a man preach, I like to see him act as if he were fighting bees."

Is the average preacher on fire with the Word? A bishop once asked one of his ministers, "How are things going in your new parish?" "Well," replied the young man, "I can't put the Thames on fire." The bishop countered, "What I want to know is, if we take you out and drop you in it, will it sizzle?"

Recently a news report told of an English rector with a peculiar problem. Every time he blew out the altar candles, his breath caught on fire. This upset his congregation, which asked him to see a doctor. It was learned he had a stomach ulcer which produced a flammable gas. When the rector blew out the candles, the gas caught on fire! Here was at least one preacher who had fire in his mouth!

Why can't a preacher of the gospel be as energetic, forceful and exercised as others who espouse a cause? Why are we not as fervent in our preaching as a Jesse Jackson? What does the labor leader or the Shiite Muslim or a Philippine communist have in fervency that a preacher of the Word does not have? How can we preachers be so calm, cool and collected when people are spiritually dying and we have only twenty minutes to raise the dead? How can we talk so unconcernedly when the nation faces a crisis? Why don't we get concerned when various sects publish heresies and when people listen to the dangerous ideas of one such as New Age proponent Shirley MacLaine?

How does a preacher come alive? Where does he or she get this enthusiasm? It does not come from giving oneself a pep talk. It is not a natural talent. Fervor comes from above. The source of excitement is in a personal relationship with God through private daily devotions. The secret is in Psalm 39:3: "As I meditated, the fire burned; then I spoke with my tongue." Fire in the pulpit results from the preacher spending time with God in daily devotions involving prayer, Bible reading, solitude and reflection. When Moses came out of his tent after meeting with Yahweh, he had to put a veil over his head because of the intensity of the radiance. When Jesus was in God's presence, he was transfigured. The tongues of fire came upon the apostles after ten days of prayer in the upper room.

If preachers are going to attract people to join the church by their enthusiastic preaching, they need to keep a daily tryst with God. In *Life Together*, Dietrich Bonhoeffer wrote,

> Since meditation on the Scriptures, prayer and intercession are a service we owe and because the grace of God is found in this service, we should train ourselves to set apart a regular hour for it.

Similarly, Joseph Sittler in *Gravity and Grace* says, "The principle work of the ordained ministry is reflection; cultivation of one's penetration into the depth of the Word so that the witness shall be poignant and strong."

To be shut up with God for an hour a day is not a prison but heaven. Monks had cells. They were not in the hell of confinement but in the heaven of God's presence. The word "cell" comes from "coelum," meaning "heaven." To be alone with God for an hour a day is an hour in heaven.

And what does one do with that hour? Albert Day in his *Autobiography of Prayer* suggests a simple procedure.

- Shut the door—silence and solitude.
- Take off your shoes—reverence in the presence of God.
- Open the window—openness to God's Spirit and message.
- Fold your hands—prayer, confession, intercession.

Persuasive Preaching

If the church is to grow, people need to be persuaded to believe in Jesus, to confess their sins, to accept forgiveness, to commit themselves to Christ and to join the church. By its dullness many a sermon today only persuades people *not* to return the following Sunday.

To be persuasive you must first be persuaded. You cannot sell a product if you do not believe in it yourself. Is the preacher persuaded that sinners need to repent or they will be lost? Is the preacher positive that the source of our personal and social ills is the result of being at odds with God? Do we preachers really believe that Christ is the ultimate answer to all our problems? A cartoon shows a discouraged pastor looking at a chart of his declining church attendance. His companion suggests, "I'm no expert, Joe, but perhaps you shouldn't close each sermon with 'But then again, what do I know?'"

If we are going to be persuasive, we must first decide what we want the congregation to believe or do. This calls for having a specific aim for the sermon. What am I going to persuade the people to do about this need or problem? If there is no need or problem, why preach about it? A defense lawyer has as his or her aim to get the client an innocent verdict. He or she therefore tries to persuade the jury that the accused is innocent. What verdict is the preacher aiming for—anything?

Persuasion implies that the congregation can and needs to respond to the preaching. Some preachers do not try to persuade. They leave that solely up to God and the Spirit. Recently one preacher ridiculed Holman Hunt's painting of Jesus standing outside a door which had no knob for him to open it. He claimed it was ridiculous to put salvation on a person's decision to open the door. Indeed, grace and faith are two sides of a coin. We are saved by grace, but we receive grace through faith. Without faith, grace is in vain. Persuasion requires response to God's grace. "Repent and be baptized"— respond! "Follow me"—respond!

Theologian Paul Tillich defined faith as "accept your acceptance." To accept is to respond. On an outdoor church bulletin board was the message "God forgives—let him!" The Philippian jailor responded, "What must I do to be saved?" The people responded to Peter's first sermon, "What shall we do?"

Recently I heard an excellent sermon on the moral condition of modern society. The preacher declared that faith in Christ was the only answer to a good society. But he stopped; he did not call the people then and there to come to faith or to renew their faith in Christ. If faith was the answer to a good society, why did he not challenge his people to go out to the highways and byways and bring people to church where they could receive faith, which in turn would result in the good life? You see, he failed to call for a response. The congregation was persuaded to do nothing!

Incarnational Preaching

A fourth characteristic of good preaching that will cause the church to grow is incarnational preaching. To be winsome, preaching must be practiced by those who preach. It does not matter if the preaching is evangelical, passionate or persuasive. If the preacher does not live his or her preaching, the preaching amounts to nothing. The old saying is still true: "What you are speaks so loudly that I cannot hear what you are saying."

In our time we have been having more than our share of preachers not living their preaching. We preachers are trying to excuse our behavior by saying we are not better than our parishioners because we, too, are human. In the news media we hear of repeated cases of preachers' marital infidelity. There is also alcoholism and even a case of murder connected with homosexuality. In the Roman Catholic Church there are presently fifty cases of priests accused of sexual abuse. A prelate called the cases "the most serious problem the church has faced in centuries."

Not only are preachers performing immoral acts, but occasionally a preacher reveals his sins to a congregation. This has been encouraged by the "story sermon" when pastors are urged to tell their "story." Is it wise to publicize our sins, to wash our linen in public? To share our shortcomings publicly can cause damage to our people's respect for the ministry. They need someone to look up to and to be a model for them. By announcing our faults the people can become disillusioned. Of course we preachers are not perfect, and we have our sins; but we need not tell our secret faults if it might result in the loss of someone's faith. Instead, we should be certain that we have close friends or associates to whom we can confess our faults and weaknesses and who can help us see areas in our lives which need to become more Christlike.

The hardest part of preaching is the living of it. To set an example is part of the job of being a leader. In his autobiography, Lee Iacocca says,

> Leadership means setting an example. When you find yourself in a position of leadership, people follow your every move. When the leader talks, people listen. And when the leader acts, people watch. So you have to be careful about everything you do.

Peter would agree. "Not lording it over those entrusted to you, but being examples to the flock" (1 Peter 5:3). Repeatedly Paul says, "Follow my example, as I follow the example of Christ" (1 Corinthians 11:1). At ordination preachers are asked, "Will you adorn the doctrine of God our Savior by a holy life and conversation?"

People are drawn to a church where the preacher is held in high regard in the community. He or she is known as a person of integrity, living his or her religion day by day. People know they can count on and trust the preacher's word outside the pulpit as well as inside it. We live in glass houses, and everyone sees that what we are in private is what we are in public. What they see relates directly to their respect for Christianity and the church.

A preacher sets the pace for the congregation. A people is no better than their pastor—"like priest, like people". If the preacher is concerned about lost souls, the people will join in witnessing. If the preacher tithes, the congregation usually is free of financial problems because they follow the preacher's example. If the preacher is interested in the community, the people will support efforts to improve local social conditions. People will join a church where the pastor says, "Be like me. Do as I do."

All things being equal, a good preacher will double the church's membership in five years. Impossible? Try it and see! Good preaching has nothing to do with church growth? It has everything to do with it! When preaching improves, watch the church grow!

Chapter 3

Is Our Preaching Authentic?

In recent years we have experienced a flood of books on preaching. Judging by the titles, we have almost a "Heinz 57" variety of preaching: biblical, liturgical, positive, pastoral, persuasive, expository, relevant, black, dynamic, experimental, worldly, life-situation, creative, integrative and narrative preaching.

Among these new books is one entitled *Authentic Preaching*. Of all the kinds of preaching possible, it seems to me that authentic preaching is the key to them all. Even though preaching may be biblical, persuasive, relevant, creative and dynamic, what good is it unless it is authentic?

First we must define "authentic." Something authentic is trustworthy, reliable, genuine and real. A hypocrite is not an authentic Christian. A counterfeit green-back is not authentic U.S. money. An antique may be a copy of an original and is, therefore, not authentic. We must ask ourselves, "Is our preaching authentic? Is it the real thing?"

Authentic Messenger?

Authentic preaching requires an authentic preacher. Is the preacher a genuine person? Is he or she real? Some preachers give the impression that they are "ET"—extraterrestrial beings who are out of this world, perched on a pedestal and carrying a holier-than-thou halo on their heads. But the preacher must be a genuine person with warts and all, like Jesus, an incarnation of the Word. In the preacher the people are to see the truth as well as hear it.

Is the preacher authentic by being sincere? Every preacher must examine his or her own heart to discern his or her motives for preaching. In Philippians, Paul refers to this problem. Some preached Christ out of envy, rivalry and partisanship and not for the love of Christ. Are we preaching to satisfy our egos? Are we, by our dynamic preaching, hoping to be appointed to the pulpit of the most prestigious church in town?

To be authentic, preachers also need to be honest. Should not preachers of the truth be truthful? Take the matter of personal illustrations used in sermons. Some claim an experience as having happened to them when actually it did not. Once in a college chapel a guest preacher told a dramatic story about his personal experience. The very next Sunday another guest preacher told the same story as though it had happened to him. Both preachers lost the congregation's respect because the people did not know which preacher to believe.

Another form of dishonesty in preaching is borrowing word for word another person's sermon without receiving permission to do so. A limerick (author unknown) states this problem well.

> There was once a preacher named Spurgey,
> Who did not approve our liturgy;
> But his sermons were fine,
> And I preached them as mine,
> And so did the rest of the clergy.

Finally, are we authentic preachers when we do not practice what we preach? A young man left the church after he watched his bishop play tennis and became disillusioned with the bishop's unchristian attitude and manner of playing. Do we excuse our lack of spiritual follow-through in our own lives by claiming we are "just human, like everybody else"? Of course, no preacher is perfect and never will be, but gross inconsistencies between proclamation and practice result in inauthentic sermons.

Authentic Message?

Authentic preaching demands an authentic message. What does it mean to have an authentic message?

To have an authentic message, preachers must be true to the text of the sermon. (This assumes, of course, the sermon has a text. If there is no text, the sermon turns into a mere address, giving good advice rather than the good news of the gospel.) If preachers are true to the text, then the sermon is the authentic Word of God. Even if preachers shout, "Thus saith the Lord" but are not true to the text, we can respond, "Thus saith *not* the Lord but the preacher!"

If the message is to be authentic, not only must we be true to the text, but the message must also be clothed in the authentic language of the people. Since communication requires the message to be received and understood by the hearers, the language must be real to the hearers. Is the language real for the congregation? Is the sermon in the preacher's language or the people's language?

C.S. Lewis tells of hearing a young preacher conclude his sermon: "And now, my friends, if you do not believe these truths, there may be for you grave eschatological consequences." After the service Lewis asked the young preacher, "Do you mean that they would be in danger of hell?" "Why, yes," the preacher replied. "Then why in the world didn't you say so?" asked Lewis.

Though he had an earned a doctorate in theology and was a university professor, Martin Luther wrote, "We must take the words from their very lips. . . . Then the people will understand." The intellectual and academic language of a professional theologian is inauthentic to the average person in the pew.

In further pursuing an authentic message, we need to ask whether the message is authentic in meeting the needs of the people. As preachers, do we preach what the people need or just what they want to hear? Do we avoid dealing with certain subjects because the people might be offended? If we were not dependent on the people's financial contributions, would we boldly tell the truth even if it made some of our people uncomfortable? Do you think the message is authentic when we aim to please people so that we can increase our popularity and fill the pews?

What about the popular preachers of our day who refuse to mention the word "sins"? People today seek success, money and approval. We can be very tempted to seek favor with them by making our message one of positive thinking only. But God's Word consists of the law and the gospel. To be authentic, the preacher's message must contain both law and gospel in proper balance.

You and I can be biblical, dynamic, creative and pastoral preachers. But if we are not authentic in each or all of these different kinds of preaching, we are nothing. Seek first to be an authentic preacher and all other kinds of preaching will be significant and edifying.

Chapter 4

What *Good* Preaching Can Do

Senate Chaplain Edward Everett Hale (1822-1909) once was asked, "Doctor, when you pray, do you look at the tragic condition of the country and then pray that the Almighty will give the senators wisdom to find solutions?" He answered, "No, I do not. I look at the senators and pray for the country."

In our day we could say the same about preachers. In the light of the tragic condition of contemporary preaching, we ought to pray not for the preacher's wisdom but for the church. This chapter's title, "What *Good* Preaching Can Do," implies that much preaching today is bad preaching. But as a method of communicating the gospel, preaching should not be despised nor discarded on the basis of today's poor preaching. Let's look at the wonderful things good preaching can do. This may motivate us to do better preaching.

God's Voice Is Heard

Through good preaching the world has a chance to hear the voice of God. Preaching is the proclamation of the Word of God. When a person truly preaches, he or she does not speak for himself or herself. The preacher is the voice of God.

The prophets had this understanding of preaching. They constantly said, "Thus saith the Lord." The biblical understanding of preaching is illustrated in the case of Hosea: "When the Lord began to speak *through* Hosea . . ." (Hosea 1:2, italics mine). This was Jesus' understanding of preaching. "He who listens to you listens to me" (Luke 10:16). Before Peter preached the people said, "Now we are all here in the presence of God to listen to everything the Lord has commanded you to tell us" (Acts 10:33). Preaching is God speaking through a human to humankind.

To the modern, sophisticated mind this may sound ridiculous. A person may say, "Imagine that person up in the pulpit speaking as God. How presumptuous!" Yes, it does seem that way, but that is exactly what true preaching is. Because it is God speaking, a preacher must study, pray and reflect long hours to be sure that it is God and not the preacher speaking. This drives a preacher to the Bible for the words of God. True preaching therefore must be biblical, and the sermon becomes an exposition, illumination and application of a text.

When people come to church, they come to hear not a human but God. They want to know who God is, where he can be found and what his will is for their lives.

If it is true that preaching is God speaking, then we can see at once that there is nothing more important in the life and work of the church than preaching. Is there anyone more important than God? Is anybody's voice more needed than God's? Every worshiper should be able to say, "I am going to hear what God has to say to me today."

Good Preaching Saves

What can good preaching do? It can save souls. This claim is about as impossible for contemporary acceptance as saying that when a person preaches, God speaks. However, this is true! Good preaching makes converts. It brings people to Christ. Lives are changed through good preaching.

How can good preaching do this? It is not in preaching as a method or technique of communication. It is not in the personality of the preacher. The power of preaching to convert people to faith in Christ is the Word of God. The Word has within it its own power to accomplish what it says. Paul calls the gospel the power of salvation. In Romans Paul says that faith comes by hearing the Word of God. The Holy Spirit is identified with the Word. The power of the Spirit is the power of the Word. As the Word is proclaimed the Spirit works on the mind and heart of the hearer. The Spirit through the Word convicts, calls and challenges a person to give his or her life to God in service to Christ.

This makes preaching a sacramental act of worship. The church really has only one sacrament, the Word. In preaching, this Word is in the oral form. In baptism and the Lord's Supper the Word is visible. Preaching and sacraments are both means of grace.

Through the Word, God speaks, guides, blesses, restores, forgives and comforts. In preaching, the Word not only speaks but acts. In this sense then preaching is an event.

In Hebrew the original word for *Word* also means "deed." When God speaks, he at the same time performs. When people worship, they place themselves under the preaching of the Word which causes them to renew their faith and relationship with Christ. True preaching saves sinners by bringing them under conviction. The Spirit in the Word enables them to believe in Jesus as the Christ. True preaching keeps believers in the church in a process of growth and nurture until they come to the fullness of the stature of Christ.

Here is a sample of what good preaching can do. One of the four thousand people present at the Easter Sunrise service at Walter Reed Hospital in Washington wrote to the preacher of the day, "I, for the most part, have been away from the church since high school. Over this time my faith in Jesus Christ waned. Both my wife and I did not feel that we needed the church, as do many other

Americans these days. Let me just say that your Easter message has rekindled the belief in Jesus Christ for me."

Good Preaching Changes Society

What can good preaching do? It can change society. Preaching has social implications. Proof of that is in the prophets of the Old Testament. No one could be more socially radical than Amos or Hosea. And throughout history preaching has inspired great social movements.

Preaching can have a powerful impact upon public policy because our social problems are basically moral problems. Every moral problem is related to a spiritual problem. If the individual can be straightened out, personal and social relations will straighten out. It may not be dramatic or exciting to stand in a pulpit Sunday after Sunday declaring the truth. Yet, the real factor of social change is in that simple preacher speaking the Word from behind the pulpit! This is where the real action is!

If only it could be seen that real, genuine and lasting social progress begins in the pulpit! Here is the place where people will be urged, motivated and inspired to love, serve and care for people. The real issue is not a matter of methods and techniques for social change. It is not a matter of where to place pressure to get social improvement. The real source of progress is in the individual heart of the person in the pew. That is where you start. It is there that we learn of God's will for humankind. When a person gives his or her heart to God, the response will be with Isaiah, "Here am I. Send me, Lord."

Worship and Good Preaching

Good preaching makes worship meaningful and relevant. In our time we think of worship and preaching as competitors. It should not be a matter of preaching or worship, but preaching and worship. To sacrifice preaching for worship would be a serious mistake. Worship without preaching can easily degenerate into liturgism, ritualism and meaningless rote. Preaching without worship is truncated. Worship without preaching is irrelevant.

Good preaching makes worship meaningful to people. The liturgy is corporate, objective and historical. This is good and serves its purpose. But worship must include preaching to make it contemporary, individualistic and personal. The sermon takes the truth of God and makes it applicable and practical to life today. The God whom we worship needs to speak to our present condition. The sermon does this. If that relevancy is lacking, worship becomes an end in itself.

In like manner preaching is preparatory for the administration of the sacraments, baptism and Holy Communion. Before we can receive these we need to be spiritually prepared.

In the case of baptism, a person must come to the sacrament with repentance and faith. What will move a person to repent of sins? It is the preaching of the law. What will produce faith in the candidate for baptism? It is the preaching of the gospel of God's love for fallen people, centered on the cross.

The same is true with the Holy Communion. To receive the promised forgiveness of sins, to have the mystical union with Christ, we must come with repentance and faith. How can we know what the Lord's Supper means except that the sermon explains it to us? What makes us sense the presence of Christ, the real presence, when the Holy Communion is celebrated? The sermon brings his presence to our attention. This adds up to the important fact that the sermon brings his presence to mind, and thus the Eucharist cannot be separated from the preaching of the Word.

Good Preaching and Your Ministry

Good preaching can fulfill the ministry of the pastor. Paul urged Timothy to fulfill his ministry. Without a faithful proclaiming of God's Word Sunday after Sunday there can be no complete fulfillment of the ministry. A minister is called to preach the Word. The church ordains the preacher to preach and administer the sacraments. In obedience to Jesus the preacher is to go and preach to every creature. When a minister preaches the Word the calling is fulfilled. After declaring the Word, preachers experience a great feeling of joy and satisfaction that they have done what was expected of them. They experience fulfillment, completion, satisfaction and peace.

Today the church is calling for good preaching. The cry is, "Give us good preaching!" Are the people not right in their demand? History proves that the church can exist without buildings, without liturgies, without choirs, without Sunday schools, without professional clergy, without creeds, without Scouts and even without women's societies. But the church cannot exist without the preaching of the Word. The time has come to restore preaching to its rightful place, to the central place. It is not just preaching that is needed; we have plenty of that. The need is for good preaching. And now we know what good preaching can do! Our challenge is to make each succeeding sermon better than the previous one!

What Great Preachers Have in Common

A colleague once asked a minister just out of seminary what he would like as an epitaph on his tombstone. He replied, "Just two words: 'He tried.'" Many years later when he became an eminent clergyman, he was asked if he would like to change his epitaph. He answered, "Yes, I want to add one word: 'He tried everything!'"

To be great in the pulpit, many of us preachers feel that we have tried everything too. We have used gadgets and gimmicks. We have screamed, condemned, praised and wept, but nothing seemed to work. We have substituted for the sermon visual aids, called in rock music groups and used lay speakers. We have told jokes to entertain the people. We have read sermons of the great and copied their ideas and/or outlines. Sometimes we spent hours preparing a sermon, and other times we spoke off the cuff.

Still nothing seemed to happen. We have despaired of ever becoming great preachers. Maybe we have even begun to doubt that preaching is an effective means of proclamation, and we have turned instead to counseling, programming or small discussion groups. We think preaching as a method has failed because we have failed as preachers. We say we have tried everything and yet nothing has worked.

Maybe our failure is that we have not yet tried everything. Maybe we have been trying the wrong things. A study of the truly great preachers of Christian history may help us.

A review of pulpit giants reveals that they had few things in common. They came from different ages with different cultures and historical settings. They used different methods of preaching. They did not have the same educational backgrounds. They belonged to different denominations. Nevertheless, these men who reached the peak in preaching had certain things in common. Anyone aspiring to success in proclaiming God's Word would be wise to notice what the giants had in common in order to emulate these great servants of God.

An Experience with God

The source of all great preaching is in the preachers' experience with God. No pre-eminent preacher in twenty centuries of preaching has been without a firsthand relationship with God in Christ. Each great preacher had his own experience and it came in a variety of ways. But in one way or another each met God face to face.

For example, John Wesley had his experience with God in a prayer meeting on Aldersgate Street. Luther met God while preparing a lecture for the university. Augustine was meditating in a garden. Francis Asbury was converted while praying with a friend in his father's barn. Billy Graham was called of God while attending a revival in a tent.

In the case of each foremost preacher there was a specific moment when God became real to them. Just like Moses, each had his burning bush; each had his vision like Isaiah in the temple. They each experienced a spiritual conversion, a complete surrender to God.

Dwight L. Moody heard a preacher say in the course of a sermon, "It remains to be seen what God can do if he can find a man who will completely surrender to him."

Moody went away determined to see what God could do with his surrendered life.

Throughout the remainder of these top preacher's lives, this initial relationship with God in and through Christ was strictly maintained. By their initial spiritual experience they became men of God. But they continued their vital relationships with God as men of prayer.

In the lives of pulpit greats, prayer was an indispensable element in their success. Each of the top preachers had a devotional life which he could not afford to neglect. Most spent not minutes but hours daily in private devotions. From the time of his college days E. Stanley Jones, for example, spent two hours a day in prayer. It is said that Richard Baxter got his sermons while he was on his knees. Like Moses, each great preacher had a tent of meeting with God outside the camp of the people.

Preaching is Primary

Every top preacher in Christian history believed in preaching. Each gave preaching top priority in his ministry. W.E. Sangster spoke for all when he said, "No pulpit has power if it lacks deep faith in the message itself and in preaching as God's supreme method in making his message known." History's greatest preachers believed in the message they proclaimed to be God's own message, and they were convinced that through the means of preaching, God would save the world. It is fair to conclude that modern preaching will not improve until preachers themselves are totally convinced that preaching is the most important work of their ministry.

For Christianity's greatest preachers, preaching was not a matter of personal choice. To preach was to live; not to preach was to disobey God's call on their lives. Each of the pulpit supermen felt a necessity to preach.

The Old Testament prophets experienced this too. There was a time when Jeremiah wished he could stop preaching, but he said, "If I say, 'I will not mention him or speak any more in his name,' his word is in my heart like a burning fire, shut up in my bones" (Jeremiah 20:9).

And that is the way it was with every great preacher: "I must preach or I will burst."

Richard Baxter confessed, "I preach as a dying man to dying men!" It was said of Macartney, "He lived to preach." Peter Marshall sensed this necessity: "I must communicate God." John Newton flatly said, "I cannot stop." Isn't this a contrast to some today who will do almost anything to get out of preaching?

Preachers of the Word

A third common characteristic among history's greatest preachers is that all, without exception, were biblical preachers. They preached the Bible because they believed that the Bible was God's Word, that God revealed himself therein and spoke to the world in and through the pages of Scripture. Their greatness was in their consideration of the Bible as a whole, giving proper balance to both Old and New Testaments. They recognized the authority of the Bible in matters of faith and life. They trusted in the power of the Bible, the power of the gospel, to save souls. That power was the power of the Holy Spirit who came to people through the oral as well as the written Word. These men were dynamic preachers, but the dynamic of their preaching was the *dunamis* of the Spirit.

For the top preachers of the centuries, preaching was an exposition of a text. They took a text and made it plain for the people so that the Word once again came alive. This text was expounded, explained, illustrated and applied to the daily lives of the people. This was one of the chief secrets of the greatest preachers of every age.

Back in the fourth century Augustine was famous as a careful expositor of the Bible. John Bunyan mastered the Bible before he started to preach. Jonathan Edwards refused to say anything in a sermon that was not supported by Scripture. Two days before Clarence Macartney died, he told his brother, who was leaving for a preaching engagement, "Put all the Bible you can in it." The secret of Moody's evangelistic work was his fidelity to the Scriptures. Campbell Morgan was known for his biblical preaching. The Reformation resulted from Luther's preaching of the truths of the Bible. He is often portrayed in pulpit robe holding up a Bible and pointing to a text.

Work without End

Great preaching never came easily. It was the result of blood, sweat and tears. Those who became paramount in the pulpit worked without end to prepare their messages, to learn the techniques of preaching and to understand both the Bible and the world. To be a biblical preacher meant long hours of hard work of exegesis and hermeneutics. It meant an examination of the original languages and consultation of dictionaries and commentaries.

The pulpit giants did not have necessarily an extensive formal education but they used their minds to the maximum. They obeyed Paul's admonition: "Do your best to present yourself to God as one approved, a workman who does not need to be ashamed" (2 Timothy 2:15). Jonathan Edwards graduated from Yale at age seventeen and later became president of Princeton. Philip Brooks was a recognized scholar of his day. Luther was a university professor. Like John Wesley, these men always kept a book in their hands, reading extensively and persistently.

Men who made it in the pulpit put hours in the preparation of their sermons. Jonathan Edwards spent twelve hours a day in his study. Paul Rees finds it necessary to spend thirty hours on each sermon. Fosdick had the rule of spending an hour of preparation for every minute he preached. If today's preachers spend an average of seven hours on sermon preparation, does that say something about today's quality of preaching?

The pulpit greats were men who studied the techniques of preaching. Every outstanding preacher made it a point to know the laws of preaching, the art and science of communicating the Word. St. Augustine wrote the very first textbook on homiletics. Brooks' lectures on preaching are still valued. Spurgeon taught young ministers how to preach. Sangster, Stewart, George Buttrick and David H.C. Read have written books on preaching.

Doesn't this have something important to say about today's preaching? Sermon preparation is often left to the tail end of the week. The average pulpiteer seldom reads more than one serious book per year. To many preachers, giving an average of twenty hours per week for sermon preparation seems a waste of time which could be spent on more practical needs. Great preaching, then and now, calls for much agony of spirit, tough digging and continual searching for illustrative materials. That is the price of great preaching.

Men of Compassion

Another common characteristic of all truly great preachers was their love of people. This concern and compassion for people resulted from their deep love of God. Each preacher's life had been transformed by Christ. Each experienced God's mercy through the forgiveness of sins and the new birth. John Newton confessed to this grace in his own epitaph: "John Newton, clerk, once an infidel and libertine, a servant of slaves in Africa, was by the rich mercy of our Lord and Savior Jesus Christ preserved, restored, pardoned and appointed to preach the faith he had long labored to destroy."

Each of these wonderful men of God had a concern for people's souls. Each wanted all men to experience the wonderful peace which comes from believing in Christ. Each carried the conviction that Christ alone can save. They believed that Jesus was *the* way to God, to heaven, to life. These great preachers were convinced that without Christ the soul died. And because of this belief, they preached with enthusiasm, vigor and zeal. They called people to repent and believe in the Christ as Savior. This was their all-consuming passion. They could say with George Whitefield, "Believe me, I am willing to go to prison and death for you. But I am not willing to go to heaven without you." This explains why the pulpit giants preached endlessly and traveled extensively. They would not leave a stone unturned until every soul was touched with the gospel. They preached to bring about decisions, not only first-time decisions to accept Christ but continuing and repeated decisions to allow Christ to be the Lord of all of life.

But this concern and compassion for people went beyond the pursuit of individual souls to surrender to Christ. The truly great preachers were concerned also about the total welfare of people: the poor, widows, orphans, derelicts and victims of an unjust and oppressive society. These preachers wanted the Word to be lived out in the world through social betterment. Since they preached Christ, they followed his example of feeding the hungry, healing the sick and championing the cause of the downtrodden.

As we have seen, the qualities found in the great preachers' lives emanated from a first-hand relationship with God, a faith in preaching, a commitment to the Bible as their textbook, countless hours of hard work in preparation for preaching and a deep love for people. To the degree that we imitate and emulate these preachers, we shall participate in the greatness of preaching.

Chapter 6

Church Renewal Through Preaching

Addressing a church convention, a Canadian pastor said, "If my own church burned, I'd stand across the street singing 'Praise God from whom all blessings flow,' with my hand out for the insurance money."

This may shock those who believe the church is not to be burned down but to be built up. However, it is a desperate way of saying that today's church needs renewal. No one can deny that the church is in a critical state. In the last two decades mainline churches have lost millions of members. Public opinion polls reveal that an increasing percentage of people believe that the church is becoming less effective and relevant to society. These facts cry out that the church needs renewal.

The church has been trying to do something about this need for renewal. Vatican II was the Roman Catholic Church's historic effort to update the church. Protestant churches have made innovations. In worship, Protestants have introduced folk masses, moved altars close to the people and permitted lay people to have a part in the leadership of the worship services. Structural changes in organization, administration and the dropping of ineffective auxiliaries have been made. Renewal has been interpreted as getting out into the world and engaging in social causes. We have tried ecumenical reforms by merging churches.

In spite of all those efforts, we see that our merged churches are no more spiritually vital than before.

New Life Through the Word

The renewal which the modern church needs is one that is internal, dealing with the spirit and heart of the church. As in Ezekiel's day, the people of God are dry, dead bones needing life. According to Ezekiel, only the Spirit of God can give this life. Thus renewal does not come from revolution, the burning down of churches, nor from renovation by rearranging ecclesiastical furniture. Instead, renewal is internal. God commanded Ezekiel, "Prophesy to these bones . . . 'Dry bones, hear the word of the Lord!'" (Ezekiel 37:4).

What does preaching the Word have to do with renewal? The Spirit comes in, speaking through the Word. It is the Spirit who creates life through God's Word, resulting in rebirth and renewal. Thus, the renewal of the church depends upon preaching the Word.

This claim can be justified by the very nature of preaching. It is none other than the very Word of God, provided that preaching is biblical and Christ-centered. Preaching is *kerygma,* the proclamation not of preachers' opinions about life, but the truth of God through a messenger called by God to perform this function. It is the good news of God's action in Jesus Christ as Lord and Savior. It is a message of truth, grace and redemption.

This understanding of preaching runs counter to a popular view that a sermon is a sharing of ideas. It is not a matter of "Tell me what you think and I'll tell you what I think." Preaching is not a dialogue between preacher and people but between God and people.

One of the new "wrinkles" in preaching is the pastor's meeting at the beginning of each week with a chosen group of lay people to discuss what might be preached the following Sunday. But according to the Bible, a preacher is to learn from God what should be said to the people. This gives a declarative element to a sermon, and it becomes a message of authority because it is God's Word to his people. The truth is to be declared whether or not it makes the people uncomfortable. The Word is to be accepted and believed because it is divine truth.

The Nature of the Word

Preaching as the key to church renewal can be justified also because of the nature of the Word that is proclaimed. The Word is of and from God, and therefore it is a Word of power. This Word has the power within it to produce what it promises. The Word of God is as good as the deed; no sooner is it said than it is done. When at the time of creation God said, "Let there be light," there was light immediately. A Roman soldier learned that his servant was healed at the very time Jesus said he was healed. In Romans, Paul says that he is not ashamed of the gospel, for it is the power of God to salvation.

What is every person's basic need? It is to be right with God. When we say that the Word has power to save, we mean that is has power to bring sinners to repentance and then to provide faith to accept the gift of grace. The Word brings this grace to humankind, and therefore it is a means of grace. For a person to be saved there must be faith to accept God's mercy. How does one come to faith? Paul teaches that faith comes by hearing the Word of God. If the church's business is to bring a person into a harmonious relationship with God, then the church must get busy preaching the Word.

The Word that is preached is not only one of power but of life. The Word is identified with the Spirit of God, and the Spirit gives life. As Ezekiel brought dead bones to life again through the preaching of the Word of the Lord, so today the preaching of God's Word will bring new life into a dead church.

The church today has all of the external factors it needs to be effective. It has tens of millions of members. Church facilities are more useful and beautiful than ever. There is an ample supply of leaders for church staffs. We are saturated with church publications, publicity, policies and programs. The one thing lacking is God's Word empowered and illuminated by his Spirit.

Biblical Preaching

In spite of our ecclesiastical machinery and promotional aids, we lack drive, spirit and life. Ask the average pastor what is wrong with the congregation and he or she will answer, "No interest." Why don't more people come to church? No interest. Why do so few people tithe? No interest. Church people lack motivation. Church programs are crippled by apathy and lethargy. Many do not care less what happens to the church or to the world.

Here is where biblical preaching is desperately needed. The Word gives life to the church. Sound biblical preaching will serve the church as a spark plug serves a motor. The biblically sound sermon will be the source of motivation and inspiration for activity.

If the church is dead, it is usually because the pulpit is dead. The church at eleven a.m. Sunday is empty because the pulpit is empty. The biblical pulpit calls for action: People are to repent, souls are to be saved, a world is to be conquered for Christ. Evil is to be eradicated from society. The motivation comes from the preaching of God's love expressed in the cross. Preaching should develop in people a sense of gratitude for what God has done for us in Christ. The sermon should challenge them to rise up and live, work and sacrifice for Christ.

Preaching is also the key to church renewal, because preaching is the best method of communication. In our day this may not be popular because preaching as a method of communication is often considered outmoded and old fashioned. Consequently, many today are looking for substitutes for preaching. A magazine article on preaching began, "Hurrah, no sermon! Let's dialogue."

One preacher displayed scenes from *Playboy* to illustrate his sermon. Another stepped into the pulpit and began to shave. One preacher has a custom of taking a dummy into the pulpit and speaking through it. Let it be said emphatically that there is nothing wrong with preaching as a technique of communication! The trouble is with the kind of preaching that is being done. Because preaching is at a low point, there is a search for sermon substitutes.

If preaching is the key to church renewal, why then is the church in the doldrums? Surely we have plenty of preaching in America. Each Sunday seventy million people listen to 230,000 preachers. The sad fact is that preaching itself is in need of renewal. How can the blind lead the blind? One minister expressed the feeling of many, "Preaching is the occupational hazard of the ministry." For many worshipers, sermon time is drop-out time. This sad condition has resulted from a general practice of offering topical sermons on current events and social problems. In most cases a text is not used, except perhaps, as a pretext. The sermons are preacher-centered rather than Christ-centered. Consequently, much of today's preaching is a waste of time.

If there is going to be any church renewal preaching, the preacher will not wish to see his or her church burned to the ground to collect the insurance money. Instead the preacher will burn with zeal for the gospel. When a young man asked John Wesley how he drew crowds, he said, "Put yourself on fire with the gospel and people will come and watch you burn up."

It is high time that we preachers became "burned up" with zeal for the gospel. Then, like the prophets, out of the ashes of her preachers the church will rise with newness of life to meet the challenges of the twenty-first century.

Chapter 7

Malpractice in Preaching

Could this happen to you as a preacher? The Sunday church service is over. You are standing at the front door greeting the people as they leave. A man says, "Preacher, I'm going to sue you for today's sermon because of malpractice in preaching." Should a preacher be held responsible for what he or she says?

It is reported that thousands of churches are now carrying malpractice insurance up to $300,000 for their pastors. Almost 6000 Methodist and 1,700 Lutheran churches are now covered by the Atlantic Mutual Insurance Company. Little is said about this coverage to discourage lawsuits.

Pastors are being sued for malpractice in ministry. A pastor in Little Rock, Arkansas, was sued for a million dollars by a husband who claimed the pastor's Bible teaching caused his wife to lose her affection for him. In Los Angeles the parents of a youth who committed suicide sued the youth's pastor, charging that he discouraged their son from seeking professional counseling. A man in Ohio sued the pastor of a faith-healing church because when the man was a child, his leg was severely burned but was not medically treated because the pastor said faith alone would cure it. For thirty years the man has been trying to repair the damage to his leg at great medical expense.

It is therefore not impossible to conceive of a worshiper saying to a pastor after a service, "I'm going to sue you for that sermon." On what grounds could a preacher be sued for malpractice in preaching?

Dull Sermons

Preachers could be sued for boring people to death by their dull sermons. Some preachers are so dull that they would give even an aspirin a headache! Their sermons cause people's minds to wander, leaving people to squirm in the pews from restlessness and boredom. During the sermon parishioners resort to counting the number of pipes in the organ screen or the number of bulbs in the chandeliers. The person who wants to sue for boredom says, "I sue you for malpractice in preaching because your sermon did not accomplish what it is supposed to: uplift, challenge and inspire me."

Why do we associate sermons with dullness? Some years ago there was a newspaper story about the discovery of an ancient holy axe in Ireland. How did they know it was a holy axe? The give-away was the sentence, "The sacred character of the axe is conjectured from the absence of an effective cutting edge." In other words, like a sermon it was dull.

Sermons are made dull by giving one generality and platitude after another. They do not get in touch with life today. For a sermon to come alive, the preacher and the content of the sermon must come alive with contemporary realities.

Heresy in Sermons

Another person coming out of the church may say, "I'm going to sue you for malpractice in preaching because of the heresy in your sermon." Is a preacher responsible for the content of the sermon and for the theology therein? If the teaching in a sermon is contrary to biblical theology and the doctrines of the church, is this not sufficient grounds for litigation?

For instance, the Bible and the church teach that in and through the incarnation the Word became flesh. Jesus is both man and God. He is the Son of God who came to reveal the truth of God and to redeem humanity from sin. As such, he alone is Savior and, according to Acts 4:12, there is salvation in no other name than Jesus.

Suppose the preacher adopts the heresy of claiming that salvation can also be found in other world religions. His sermon says, "Those who say that there is no salvation outside Christianity are dogmatic diehards." The preacher goes on to say that the historical Jesus did not teach that he was God. Moreover, the preacher claims that the incarnation was a myth.

A person listening to this kind of theology has a right to sue for malpractice in preaching. The charge could be: "You have taken away my Lord and I do not know where to find him. You have destroyed my confidence and assurance that Jesus is my Lord and Savior."

Abuse of Text

Another worshiper may charge, "You were not true to the text of your sermon. You said one thing and the text said another. The theme of your sermon did not harmonize with the theme of the text. A preacher at least ought to say exactly what the text says and means. You used the text merely as a springboard for your own ideas."

It is a serious thing to charge a preacher with the non-use, misuse or abuse of the text. How many preachers could be sued for malpractice for misusing God's Word?

Suppose another worshiper says, "I came to church this morning full of hope that I would be helped. I have a problem and I was hoping to hear a solution. I also have questions that need answering. But what did I get today from your sermon? Frankly, I got nothing. A minister is to help his or her people. I am going to sue you for malpractice because your preaching made me worse off than before I came to church."

In every congregation there are as many needs as there are people. To fail people in their need is reason for a lawsuit.

What can keep preachers from being sued for malpractice in preaching? Our protection is not in an insurance policy, but in our fidelity to God's Word. The apostle Paul advises, "Preach the Word" (2 Timothy 4:2). The Word can do no harm but only help, enrich and edify every listener.

Chapter 8

Can We Make too Much of the Sermon?

Is the sermon the climax of the worship service? Is it the primary reason for coming to church on a Sunday? For some people it is. When I began my ministry, people would refer to "going to preaching" rather than going to church or to worship. Do we go to church to hear preaching, or do we go to church to worship?

"Going to preaching" would seem to harmonize with the new thrust in the eighties of the primacy of preaching. It is a reaction to the sixties when it was claimed that the sermon was dead as an effective means of communicating the gospel. Once again congregations are appealing for good preachers. Religious publishers are flooding the market with books of sermons, Bible commentaries for preachers and books about preaching. Church officials and editors of church periodicals are calling for a new emphasis on preaching. Recent polls indicate that preachers are once again putting preaching on the top of the list of their priorities, and they say that preaching brings them the most satisfaction in their ministries.

In keeping with this emphasis on sermons, some people claim that the sermon is the climax of a worship service. Are we going from one extreme to the other, from making too little to making too much of the sermon?

I find myself in an awkward position on this question. For almost twenty years I have been teaching and, I hope, persuading seminary students that preaching should be the top priority in their ministries. Out of fear of going to another extreme, I am forced to raise a caution flag by insisting that the sermon is not everything. We must maintain a balance and a perspective between sermon and sacrament, preaching and worship, proclamation and liturgy.

In attempting to answer the question of whether or not the sermon is the climax of the worship service, we need to consider the question in two situations: a regular worship service and a Communion service.

The Climax of a Worship Service

Is the sermon the climax of a regular worship service? There are those who claim that it is. For them the sermon is like the pinnacle of a pyramid. All that precedes the sermon is introductory to it. Consequently the sermon is placed last in the order of worship, followed by a benediction and a hymn. It is like the order of an ecclesiastical procession: the clergy, followed by a bishop, come at the end of the procession. The last is most important. The sermon coming last makes it of primary importance in the service. But making the sermon the climax of a worship service can put too much pressure on the preacher: If the sermon fails the worship is ruined. This is a burden that should not be placed on a preacher, because in spite of a preacher's best efforts, there are times when he or she blows it. When the sermon is not up to par the worshiper should be able to gain strength and comfort from the whole worship experience.

Moreover, when we make the sermon the climax of a regular worship service we abuse the worship service. We use worship as a means to the end, which is preaching. Worship should not be put at the service of the sermon. Rather, worship is the end in itself.

Also, making the sermon the climax of the service indicates a misunderstanding of the nature of a sermon in relation to worship. A sermon is but one aspect of worship; it is a sacramental act of worship. There are two basic elements in worship: sacrificial and sacramental. In the former the worshiper responds to God; in the latter God speaks to his people. The sermon is God speaking to people through a person who faithfully proclaims the Word. It is a listening time of worship. Thus true worship is more than listening; it is also responding. When, then, is the climax of a worship service? For me, the climax comes after the sermon when the worshiper responds to God's presence and Word by dedicating or re-dedicating his or her life to God. We can listen to God's Word and do nothing about it. We can praise and pray, but God wants more than lip service. The climax comes when with Isaiah we say, "Here am I. Send me!" (Isaiah 6:8).

The Sermon and Communion

What about the worship service with Holy Communion? What is the climax of a Communion service? For those who believe and accept the real presence of Christ in the elements of bread and wine, the climax of a Communion service is not in the sermon but in the mystical union of Christ and the believers. This personal union takes place when the bread and wine are received by faith as the reality of Christ's true presence. The believer and Christ become one. This oneness is the climax of a Communion service.

This raises the question about the place of the sermon in a Communion service. Should there even be a sermon? If so, should it be a brief meditation or homily?

A sermon should never be separated from the sacrament. Sermon and sacrament are two sides of the coin of God's Word. They need each other. The sacrament is the fulfillment and consummation of the preached Word.

On the other hand, the sacrament needs the sermon for several reasons. The sermon declares the meaning of Communion. Through the Spirit's working through God's Word the sermon creates and replenishes faith, which enables the communicant to receive the benefits of the sacrament. The sermon makes the objective sacrament personal, subjective and applicable to the communicant's life. The sermon prevents the sacrament from falling into the error of "ex opera operato."

Preaching a sermon during a Communion service presents a practical problem of time. In some churches the extra liturgy and administration cause the service to exceed an hour. Parishioners are accustomed to an hour of worship, and many are unhappy if the service goes beyond the hour. This length problem encourages some preachers to omit the sermon or to limit it to a few minutes. If Holy Communion is celebrated frequently, people are deprived of full-length sermons and the proclaimed Word is slighted. The sermon is not the place to cut. The musical "special" or the children's sermonette or the announcements which have been printed already in the church bulletin could be eliminated. Also, much time is wasted in the administration of the elements. Time could be saved if the journey to and from the altar rail were streamlined and a continuous table introduced.

If we make the sermon the sole or primary reason for going to church, we are making too much of the sermon. The primary reason for going to church is to worship God. The climax of a service is an experience with God. The sermon, however, is an indispensable factor.

Part II

The Messenger of Preaching

Preaching is an act of daring, and only the man who would rather not preach and cannot escape from it ought to ever attempt it.

—Karl Barth

Chapter 9

The Discipline of Devotions

Like the nation, the church is experiencing a crisis of leadership. According to Thielicke, *The Trouble with the Church* is the trouble with preaching. The trouble with preaching is the trouble with preachers who have little or no devotional life.

To be adequate and effective leaders, ministers need to be spiritual persons. Otherwise they are salt without savor, leaven without potency and lanterns without oil. They know about Jesus but do not know him personally.

This lack of ministerial spirituality is often due to the neglect of a personal devotional life. For the laity private devotions are necessary because one hour of worship per week is insufficient for adequate spiritual growth. For the clergy private devotions are doubly necessary because their leadership of worship does not allow them to fully worship in a receptive sense.

Some would say with William James, "I have no living sense of communion with God." One American college reports that ninety-three percent of their pre-ministerial students say, "I have no devotional life." A seminarian confessed, "The greatest difficulty I seem to be having is being aware of my own spirituality. I don't seem to have enough resources of faith to draw on in this vocation. I don't seem to have adequate spiritual disciplines to continually nourish that faith. My prayer and worship life does not seem to feed my own needs in this situation."

This dearth of spirituality is being recognized outside the church. Over a period of four years a secular foundation gave more than one million dollars in grants to American theological schools for the development of the spiritual lives of ministers. When the secular world asks the leadership of the church to be more spiritual, it is time to hang our heads in shame.

The church is calling for pastors who are spiritual leaders. Some years ago a study was made of five thousand Lutherans in America, both clergy and lay people, concerning their views of the ministry. Seventy-seven characteristics in ten areas were considered. The report revealed that the most important element in ministry was a pastor's faith and an awareness of God as the center of life. Of all seventy-seven ministerial qualities, a pastor's devotional life was considered of first importance.

Enemies of Personal Devotions

Our day and age is not conducive to private devotions and the cultivation of spirituality. This is the generation which has little sympathy for the development of spirituality. The emphasis is upon the secular rather than upon the sacred, upon the natural rather than upon the supernatural, upon the immanence of God rather than upon his transcendence, upon people rather than upon God, upon the horizontal rather than upon the vertical plane of life. Our secular world has no place for private devotions to nurture the spiritual life. It frowns on prayer and solitude.

It is said that modern people no longer feel the need for God or spiritual resources, that they have the intellectual and industrial capacity to fulfill all their needs. They have medicine for their health, the ability to extend life by transplanting organs, education which doubles their knowledge every ten years, wealth to meet their material needs and psychiatry for their souls. What more could people want? Why would they need God or take time for personal devotions to cultivate a closer relationship with him?

Radical theology is a second enemy of private devotions. If God is dead or absent, there is no sense in spending time with a non-reality. Private devotions are undergirded by a biblical theology which affirms that God is. He is not an abstract principle nor an impersonal force but a personal God with whom we can communicate by prayer. God is approachable and prayers are offered in and through his Son. Private devotions are built upon the fact that humanity was created by God for God and to be in continual fellowship with him. A human was made a living soul capable of entering communion with God. Thus people instinctively and naturally seek God and pray to him.

Private devotions are necessary for the maintenance and development of this relationship with God because, just as a picture can fade, contact with God can be lost, faith can weaken and love for God can die. The goal of the devotional life is to unite in spiritual oneness with God and to live and reflect that oneness in every activity of life. Success is attained when we can say with St. Paul, "I no longer live, but Christ lives in me" (Galatians 2:20).

Another enemy of spirituality for the minister is the busyness of the modern church which leaves no time for devotions. The average pastor is caught up in the busy program of the church. For many the successful minister is one about whom people proudly say, "He does not have a minute for himself."

The pastor is on the go from morning until night. Pastors rush from one meeting to the next. Jesus did not emphasize busyness; in fact he criticized Martha for being caught up in activity and commended Mary for sitting down with him to talk about things of eternal importance. The running person rejects quietness and stillness as Isaiah said, "In repentance and rest is your salvation, in quietness and trust is your strength, but you would have none of it. You said, 'No, we will flee on horses'" (Isaiah 30:15,16).

In a world of such enemies of the devotional life, a minister is compelled to fight for his or her right to be alone with God. If a pastor does not do it voluntarily, maybe he or she should follow the advice of a Presbyterian minister in Indiana who wrote,

> Take him off the mailing list, lock him up with his books and his Bible. Slam him down on his knees before texts, broken hearts, the flippant lives of a superficial flock and the holy God. Throw him into the ring to box with God all the night through. Let him come out only when he is bruised and beaten into being a blessing. Rip out his telephone, burn up his ecclesiastical success sheets, refuse his glad hand and put water in the gas tank of his community buggy. Give him a Bible and tie him in his pulpit and make him preach the Word of the living God. (Floyd Shafer, *Christianity Today*, March 27, 1961).

Values of Private Devotions

The history of the church shows that the progress of the church was the result of the piety of her leaders. The church began on Pentecost when the disciples received the Holy Spirit. The Holy Spirit brought new life, zeal and courage to confess Christ in a hostile world. We often forget, however, that before the Spirit was received, the disciples were instructed to wait and pray for the Spirit. For ten days they met together in Jerusalem for prayer. If the church today is to experience another Pentecost, our ministers must spend time in personal devotions.

The monastic movement's secret to success in the Middle Ages was its schedule of daily devotions. Worship was central in monastic life. Seven services of prayer were held daily. Solitude and contemplation were emphasized. The monastic movement brought a new spiritual depth to the Christian world.

The Reformation had its source not so much in the intellectual labors of the Reformers but in their spiritual lives. Before he became a reformer, Martin Luther was interested in mysticism and praised the mystic, John Tauler (1300-1361). Luther was an Augustinian monk who gave many hours daily to prayer and meditation. It was in the solitude of a monk's cell that Luther struggled with his soul. It was in the Black Tower of the monastery when he discovered a gracious God in the Scriptures. For almost two years Luther cloistered himself in the Wartburg castle—meditating, praying, studying and translating—before he resumed the leadership of the Reformation.

It is quite obvious that the church's present progress depends upon the spiritual life of her clergy. The church today, as always, gets her power from the spiritual life of her pastors. Because of the poor spiritual condition of the average church today, the church has about as much influence on society as yesterday's newspaper and less influence than a civic club.

But where churches have a depth of faith and a closeness to God and are under the leadership of pastors who are living daily in God's presence, there is a source of spiritual power radiating throughout the community. From this spirituality in the church comes a compassionate concern for the welfare of all people.

Private devotions are indispensable for faithful pastors. It is daily food for their souls. Few lay people realize that pastors have no Sundays for spiritual refreshment. Ministers are always giving—themselves, ideas, counsel, sympathy and love. On Sundays they literally pour themselves out to their congregations as they lead in worship and preach the Word. At the end of the day they are physically and emotionally exhausted.

When do pastors worship? When do they get their souls filled? What they do not get in public worship they must get in private devotions. In their daily tryst with God their souls are built up in faith and God refreshes them with his presence. Without this time for devotions pastors would be shallow and starved in the inner man. Thus the hour spent with God is the pastor's finest hour of the day.

Private devotions are valuable for ministers,

moreover, because they give conviction and power for preaching. Sermons are born in the quiet hour of the prayer room. The Word a person preaches must be a living power, becoming part of them, producing new life in them. Their preaching must be an expression of their personal religious life. In personal devotions the Word becomes united with a living personality and embodies itself in the life of the preacher. When the Word comes to a pastor's heart he or she speaks with a new vigor, a deep conviction and a new power. Powerful preaching depends upon deep conviction. Convictions come out of prayer. It is not surprising that great preachers have always been people of prayer.

Personal devotions are also valuable because they help preachers live up to their preaching. We preachers have our own deadly sins—religiosity and profes- sionalism, for example. Jesus denounced the profes- sional preachers of his day, the Pharisees.

Who is to correct a preacher? If preachers repent, it will be during their private devotions when they examine themselves in the light of the Word of God. It is in this very private time of soul-searching that ministers face their pride, professionalism, self-centeredness and sloth. Ministers find that private devotions give them the inner braces they need against the pressures of temptations. In their prayer lives, pastors beg that after they have preached to others, they might not be castaways.

Ministers find that by living constantly in the presence of God they begin to reflect the character of Christ. They want to be rich in grace, deep in faith, great in love and "little Christs" in their communities. In their daily devo- tions ministers get the motivation to be what they ought to be. They gain strength for their unending tasks and a desire to live wholly for God. In the quiet time of private devotions ministers open up their lives to the Holy Spirit who fills them with power and insight.

The Discipline of Private Devotions

If private devotions are going to have the values this

chapter has mentioned, ministers must put themselves under the discipline of private devotions. Effective, helpful and productive devotions do not result from haphazard, now-and-then or whenever-I-feel-like-it attitudes and practices. A pastor must accept rules for personal devotions and religiously abide by them.

One element of the discipline is keeping a stated time for private prayer. The devotional period must receive top priority in a minister's daily schedule. The period needs to be kept daily without fail except for an emergency in the family or parish. If we realize how essential devotions are to the success of ministry, we would place the devotional period as a daily "must" in our crowded schedule.

The place for daily devotions is important because it must be a place free from distractions, disturbances and interruptions. In our increasingly crowded world, where can a place like this be found? A deliberate attempt must be made to isolate one's self from the world, family and church. One minister had a retractable staircase. After he went to his study, he pulled up the staircase. When telephone calls came, the church secretary truthfully said, "Dr. So-and-so cannot be reached at this time." An old pastor once advised a young man just beginning his ministry, "Spend a certain time each day away from your family and friends in quiet, where you can study your Bible, pray and wait for God to speak. In that way you will grow in depth and not in shallowness."

A third element of the discipline of private devotions is silence. A person may find a place to be alone, but unless it is a quiet place, the solitude will not be effective. Silence is essential for profitable communion with God. The world and its noise must be shut out so that a person can hear God. In our busy, noisy culture, this becomes a problem. Where can you find a place that is free from the ring of the telephone, the noise of the streets, the blare of the radio or television, the calls or cries of the family? Why is silence needed? Silence enables us to concentrate upon the divine voice. God speaks to us in a "still, small voice." When things are quiet, the silence become alive with messages from God.

The Content of Private Devotions

If ministers decide that from henceforth they will set aside an hour at the beginning of each day for the development of their spiritual lives, what will they do with that hour so that it will be as fruitful as possible? Each person must work out an agenda that best suits his or her personal needs. But there are elements that must be included for maximum benefit.

The devotional period includes prayer. The first part of the hour might be spent in conversation, verbal or non-verbal, with God through Christ. It is a time to get acquainted, to settle down, to get accustomed to the "other" world of the Spirit. Through the use of devotional helps we focus the mind on spiritual matters and begin to think spiritually. Many devotional guides for ministers are available. Here is an opportunity to become acquainted with and to use classic devotional materials of past ages.

The prepared prayers of the past should conclude with a minister's own prayers. He or she engages in intercessory prayer in behalf of family, friends, parishioners and the world. A wise pastor will use the membership roll of the congregation as his prayer list, taking several names each day for prayer.

Through prayer pastors may do their most effective work. St. John of the Cross advises,

> Let men, eaten with activity, who think they are rousing the world by their preaching or other exterior work, reflect here a moment. They will understand without difficulty that they would be more useful to the church and more agreeable to the Lord, without speaking of the good example they would spread around them, if they gave more time to prayer and the exercises of the interior life (quoted by Wheeler in *The Priest and His Prayer*, 1939).

In the hour of devotion ministers will make provision

for solitude. Now that they have talked with God, both with or without devotional aids, they allow God to talk with them. They are silent and alone with God. They are relaxed and receptive. How does God speak to us at a time like this? He may speak to us in various ways, but he speaks primarily in and through the Scriptures. In a letter to a friend, St. Jerome asked, "Dost thou pray? Thou art speaking with the Bridegroom. Dost thou read? He is speaking with thee." We take our Bibles and read them devotionally, not in search of texts or illustrations. We let the Bible speak to us as it will. Out of this solitude comes creative ideas. When students asked Carl Sandburg how to become a writer, he answered, "All you need is a bit of solitude and a bit of prayer."

Meditation is another essential part of private devotions. After reading the Word we reflect on what we read. Meditation is the time for thinking, for reflecting. Of course, this calls for discipline of the mind, for naturally we do not want to think; it is too difficult! A famous churchman said to his son, "If you have only three minutes to give to Bible reading in the mornings, give one minute to reading and two minutes to thinking about what you read." Thinking is prerequisite to successful activity later in the day. You think through your problem, know what you are going to do and say and why. Then you do it with singleness of mind and purpose. General MacArthur once said that he could not win a battle if he had not preceded it with at least one hour of thought.

Enrichment reading should be a part of the daily devotional hour. The hour may be closed with a short period for reading material that will build us up in the faith and enlighten our minds. Here is an opportunity to read the classics, devotional books that speak to the inner life and a book on theology.

If we include these elements in our devotional period, we will come out of the hour feeling it was the shortest hour of the day. It is not only the shortest but it also proves to be the most delightful, creative and productive hour of the day. Reluctantly we leave the hour of devotions for parish duties. With mind and heart attuned to God, with spirit refreshed and mind enriched, we are now ready to go down the mountain of prayer to the valley of human needs.

John Baillie tells the story of a man in India richly attired and leading a fine horse who was attacked by a troop of robbers. "Brother, who are you?" they asked. "I'm So-and-so, the servant of Such-a-one," he replied, "and I am taking this horse to my master's son as a gift from his uncle." Then they seized him and carried off his horse. Later in the day, he fell in with another troop of robbers who likewise asked him who he was. "I am So-and-so, the servant of Such-a-one," he replied, "and I carry to my master's son as a gift from his father a gold chain." They found the chain, took it and most of his clothes, but let him go. At last he reached his destination and presented himself to his master's son who, seeing a limping, footsore man wearing only a ragged loincloth, asked him in astonishment who he was. "I am So-and-so, the servant of Such-a-one, who is your father," he replied, "and I bring to my master's son this gift." And so saying he took from his armpit the great pearl, now called the Mountain of Milk, which to this day is chief among the Amirs of that land. For a productive and blessed ministry the one thing a minister cannot give up is his or her devotional life. It is the pearl of great price for a successful ministry.

Chapter 10

Are You Called to Preach?

Is the ministry a calling or a career? Is the gospel ministry a vocation similar to any job, a way of making a living? Or is the ministry to be considered a profession such as medicine, law, nursing and teaching? Is the ministry something we decide upon or is it something God calls us to do?

In recent years we are hearing little about the ministry as a calling of God and more about it as a profession and career which we decide to enter and leave when we choose to do so. To think of the ministry as only a job may be a major reason for the high rate of drop-outs and burn-outs in today's ministry. According to the Alban Institute, "One of every five clergy in the United States is burned out" (Gustav Niebuhr, *Atlanta* Constitution, October 1, 1988). One-third of the clergy admit to considering the possibility of leaving the ministry and twenty to thirty percent do leave it.

If you are called, are you called to the ministry in general, with preaching as one item in the job description? Or, are you called primarily to preach the Word and administer the sacraments with the other tasks such as administration, worship leadership, counseling and pastoral care as secondary functions? Indeed, one may feel called to the ministry of music, education, counseling or visitation. In this case, preaching is a side issue, if an issue at all. What you do about preaching, what priority you give preaching and the amount of preparation you spend on sermons will depend on whether you are called primarily to preach or to another phase of ministry.

Sure of It?

Are you called to preach? Are you absolutely sure of it? Are you positive that this is what God wants you to do with your life? And if you do not preach would you feel unfulfilled, dissatisfied and miserable? With Paul can you say, "Woe to me if I do not preach the gospel!" (1 Corinthians 9:16)?

If your answer is, "Yes, without a shadow of a doubt," then you must preach. If it is God's will for you to preach, you must learn how to do it. It must be your life's ambition, then, to become the very best possible preacher according to your talents and training.

As a parish pastor you are called upon to preach time after time. One cannot be a pastor of a congregation without preaching. Every Sunday approximately thirty percent of your members will gather to hear you preach as a part of the worship experience. When you confirm the youth of the parish, you will preach a confirmation sermon. When you join couples in marriage, you will preach a wedding homily. When you bury your people's dead, a sermon is expected to give hope and comfort to the sorrowing.

Your counseling will depend upon your preaching. When the disturbed with their nagging problems hear you preach with love and understanding of human problems, they will call for a counseling appointment. Your entire ministry depends on your preaching. For a fruitful ministry, you have to learn how to preach effectively.

Why This Claim?

Why such an emphasis on effective preaching? Because at your ministerial ordination you were authorized to preach the Word and administer the sacraments. This special call makes a pastor's ministry different from and superior to all other forms of ministry.

Of course there is the ministry of all Christians which begins with the ordination of baptism. All Christians are, in a sense, ministers and are ordained to serve in various capacities in the church and world. There are ministries of music, education and service. Each person's secular vocation is a calling to serve God. However, the call to preach the Word and administer the sacraments is God's highest calling.

This does not mean that the ordained minister is higher, more holy or superior to the laity. It is not the minister as a human being that is greater. Rather, it is the Word and sacraments that are of supreme value and importance. The ordained person does not think he or she is better than other servants of God. In contrast, the ordained minister feels humble and unworthy to bear this great responsibility and privilege. To stand up and preach usually means for some an upset stomach, sleepless Saturday nights, many hours of hard labor, agony and weak knees. Unless called, hardly anyone would go through all of this to preach. He or she needs to place total confidence in God, because a minister of the Word often feels totally inadequate for the high and holy task of preaching.

Why So Important?

Why is the ministry of preaching the Word and administering the sacraments so important? It is not in the person of the preacher but in the nature of the Word. Preaching is the oral Word of God. The Word is God's own revelation and message to the world. God promised that his proclaimed Word would never return void. There is divine power inherent in the Word, the "power of God for the salvation" (Romans 1:16). The Word is the bread of life that strengthens and nurtures.

Preaching the Word and administering the sacraments constitute God's most important and essential ministry. Only the Word and sacraments can bring sinners to repentance and cause God and people to be reconciled.

Are you called to preach? If you are positively certain that you are called, more certain than of anything else in your life, then you must learn to preach the Word and rightly administer the sacraments. What a holy calling you have! Do you say to God, "What didst thou find in me that thou hast dealt so lovingly?" You say that you have been called to preach? Go for it!

Then you will agree with Martin Lloyd-Jones about the ministry of preaching: "There is nothing like it. It's the greatest work in the world, the most thrilling, the most rewarding, and the most wonderful."

Chapter 11

The Divine Dimension in Preaching

When you preach, do people hear you or God? When Paul preached the people of Thessalonica heard God: "When you received the word of God, which you heard from us, you accepted it not as the word of men, but as it actually is, the word of God" (1 Thessalonians 2:13).

The missing element in much of today's preaching is the divine dimension. We hear a human rather than the divine speaking through the pastor. This is the root cause of today's ineffective sermons and consequently a cause of the mainline churches' decline in numbers and influence. People do not want to hear only what the preacher thinks about the basic issues of life, nor do they want to know only what the preacher thinks or believes or has experienced.

They say, "After all, you are just another human being, and your opinion may be no better than mine. As people in the pew, we want a word from God. Like Habakkuk, preachers need to go to the tower, stay with God a while, and learn what God has to say to us. You must then come to us on Sunday and tell us what God says about our pressing problems and needs."

That many of us preachers are speaking only for ourselves is shown by our repeated phrases: "I think," "I suggest," "I hope," "I believe," "It seems to me," "I had an experience" or "Let me tell you my story." People in the pews are saying to us, "Sermon-time is not the time for sharing your ideas but for telling us what God has to say about our condition."

When a preacher is speaking for God, he or she must slip into the background. If the preacher speaks God's Word, we soon forget whether the preacher is male or female, black or white, whether vestments are worn or not, whether the church is large or small, whether there is a pulpit-centered or a divided chancel, or whether the preacher is Catholic or Protestant. These things are relatively insignificant. The Word is being heard. God is speaking and the accouterments accompanying his or her message are incidental. The people see only Christ and hear only the voice of God.

Methodist Bishop Earl Hunt tells of preaching in his home church. After the sermon the school superintendent handed him a paper with three sentences on it.

> He stood *before* the cross and spoke; the people saw him, heard a voice, but heeded not. He stood *beside* the cross and spoke; the people saw him and the cross, heard the voice, but heeded not. He stood *behind* the cross and spoke; the people saw not the preacher, but the cross, heard the voice of Jesus and were saved.

How God Speaks

A sermon is the proclamation of God's Word by one ordained by the church to do so. At ordination the candidate is given the charge and authority to preach the Word and administer the sacraments. As such, the ordained person is not only God's spokesperson but is the official voice of the church.

This means that an ordained preacher can rightly say, "Listen, people, I am the voice of God to you." Isn't this what the prophets were saying when they declared, "Thus saith the Lord"? Is this the height of presumption—a human speaking for God? Who is really speaking in a sermon—you or God? Would God really say what you said last Sunday?

We are called and ordained to preach the Word of God. To preach the Word is to preach the Scriptures, for they record the Word. What God has to say to us today he says in and through the Bible which has its center and heart in Christ, the incarnate Word. To preach the Bible truly is to preach Christ.

But what part of the Bible do we preach? It is the part which is known as the text. Therefore, almost without exception, a sermon in which God speaks has a text, for it is part of God's Word, the truth God wants his people to hear. What we preachers do with the text determines whether God or a human is speaking in the sermon. The cardinal sin of a preacher is the non-use, misuse or abuse of the text. This is tampering with God's Word.

Thus the preacher's first task is to choose a good text, for not all possible texts are well-suited to be sermon themes. "So I commend the enjoyment of life, because nothing is better for a man under the sun than to eat and drink and be glad" (Ecclesiastes 8:15) is one such example. Through the lectionary let the church suggest a proper text for preaching your next sermon.

Next, it is necessary to properly understand and use the text. This calls for study of it. Through exegesis, learn what the text really says. After a thorough exegesis comes hermeneutics. What does this text mean? Do you understand it? Since many sermons reveal the lack of correct exegesis, this is an exceedingly important step in allowing God to speak to the people.

When does the congregation hear the text? Must the people wait until a reference is made in the course of the sermon to learn that there is one? Today many sermons do not announce a text at the beginning even if there happens to be one. In the past it was said that a Roman Catholic sermon began with a doctrine and a Protestant sermon began with a text. The Protestant practice needs to be reinstated. Before the introduction, the text needs to be read from the pulpit.

When the text is announced, the congregation learns the source and basis for the sermon. During the intro-duction the text needs to be repeated for the sake of emphasis. In textual and expository sermons the text is repeated at each main point of the outline because it provides the main points. It is the preacher's job never to let the congregation lose sight of the text. Generally it is announced before the sermon starts and is given throughout the sermon as the theme and main points are mentioned. In very rare cases the text may come later in the sermon, even in the conclusion as a summary of the sermon's truth.

If the people are to hear God speak, the text must be allowed to speak. It is possible to announce a text and use it merely as a pretext, as a decoration of the sermon or as a springboard for one's own opinions. But the cardinal principle in biblical preaching is to let the text speak the truth of God through its theme and main points. At each division of the theme the text should be quoted according to the main point. If this is done, the people will get at least one thing from the sermon: the text. If they get the text, they will have heard the Word.

The Difference

When the text is properly used in a sermon the preacher can truly say, "Thus saith the Lord." When God speaks through and in the sermon, it makes a world of difference in preaching.

Now we understand the role of a preacher. We preachers are not speaking to entertain our people. We do not speak to win a popularity contest. We do not soft-pedal our message so that crowds will come to hear us tell them only what they want to hear. We do not refrain from mentioning, exposing or condemning sin for fear of offending our hearers. It is not our sole purpose to make people feel good and comfortable when the Word would make them uncomfortable. Did David feel good when

Nathan said to him, "You are the man"? Were the people comfortable when Amos called them "cows of Bashan"? Or when Jesus called the Pharisees whited sepulchers and sons of snakes? As Paul wrote, we do not preach to please people with itching ears but to call them to repentance and faith. Preaching is God making an appeal through us to return to him. Our responsibility as preachers is to be so faithful in declaring the Word that people will hear God speaking to them. Our role is to be the mouthpiece of God, and the success of a preacher is not in the size of his or her congregation but in faithfulness to the Word.

Should a preacher then be held responsible for the effects of truth declared? A preacher can say with Jeremiah,

> As for me, I am in your hands; do with me whatever you think is good and right. Be assured, however, that if you put me to death, you will bring the guilt of innocent blood on yourselves . . . for in truth the Lord has sent me to you to speak all these words in your hearing (Jeremiah 26:14-15).

A preacher can rightfully say to a congregation, "If you don't like what I preach from God's Word about tithing or about adultery or about race relations, don't blame me. This is God's message. You have to take your objection to him!"

When people feel that they are hearing God speak to them in the sermon, they will flock to the church services to hear what God has to say to them. People will go where they are fed, for most are spiritually hungry.

One day we stopped at a restaurant in Gatlinburg, Tennessee, for breakfast. The restaurant was packed and a line of waiting customers extended for a city block. It was a cold morning, and the management kindly distributed free coffee to the waiting diners to help keep them warm.

Why would people wait so long out in the cold? It was because of the restaurant's quality food and service.

While waiting I remarked to my wife, "When people line up like this to enter a church to hear God's Word, it will be the Millennium." People will go where they are fed. When the Word is truly preached, they receive the bread of life for their hungry souls. Then they will respond, "Thanks be to God for his Word." They will leave the church service certain that God spoke to them that day. When God speaks, people will come to listen.

The next time you preach, will the people hear you or God?

Chapter 12

How Much of Self in a Sermon?

A sermon can be, and often is, a temptation for a preacher to preach "himself." The pulpit arrangement sometimes encourages this. For two Sundays I was the supply preacher for a Miami church. Before the service a lay leader explained that I was to go into the pulpit during the hymn before the sermon, attach a microphone to my robe, punch certain buttons that would dim the lights in the chancel and nave and turn on the two spotlights focused on the pulpit. Then I would come into prominence, and the people's eyes and ears would turn toward the pulpit.

I felt like I was saying, "Now listen to me, everybody! I am in the driver's seat and no one answer back!" This approach could make any preacher come to use the pulpit as a barricade against criticism from the nave. It can become an ego trip.

In an interview, television talk-show star Johnny Carson confessed that in a social group he is shy and insecure, but when he is on television or the stage, he is very confident. He explained that when he is performing he feels he is in control, and he can say what he wants to say without fear of anyone's contradiction. Many a preacher shares Carson's experience.

The congregation can contribute to this exaltation of the preacher. Many come to church to hear Dr. So-and-so preach. They do not come primarily to worship or to hear God speaking in the proclamation of the Word. One Sunday Henry Ward Beecher had a guest preacher. When visitors learned that Beecher was not preaching some left. The visiting preacher announced, "All those who came to worship Henry Ward Beecher may now withdraw; all who came to worship God may remain."

The problem is that we cannot preach without involving ourselves to some extent. The question is how much of self is appropriate and helpful in the proclamation of the gospel? There is truth to Philip Brooks' classic definition of a sermon: "truth through personality." It is not truth *in* personality nor truth *of* personality, but truth *through* personality. A preacher uses his or her person as a mouthpiece for God's Word, and the effectiveness of the Word depends to some degree upon the effectiveness of the preacher. Moreover, the preacher serves as a window through which the people see the truth and grace of God. Every preacher must answer the question: How much of myself should be in a sermon?

Too Much of Self

In recent years the trend is to put too much of self in a sermon. We have ignored Paul's confession to the Corinthians: "For we do not preach *ourselves*, but Jesus Christ as Lord" (2 Corinthians 4:5, italics mine). One reason for preaching ourselves is the topical preaching used commonly now, relying on a biblical text as a source of the sermon. Furthermore, in recent years seminarians have been taught that pastors should identify with their parishioners. They are told, "Be one of them. Let them see you as a human being. Tell them about your doubts, struggles and sins." The present trend in preaching is to tell "your story." In a recent novel a character commented, "When his clerical collar comes off, a priest is a man."

But self-centered preaching is harmful because the congregation hears and sees us rather than Christ. A true sermon is God speaking through a person, and is not a speech about God as a preacher knows him.

An "I"-centered sermon can be only good advice and not good news. It may be a word of testimony but not a Word of God. With a preacher-dominated sermon, the people will not be fed the bread of life and they will go home disappointed, for they came with the request, "Sir, we wish to see Jesus."

The Right Use of Self

So far we have seen the wrong use of self in a sermon. Is there a right use, a use that is legitimate and appropriate? The answer is "Yes." The right use of self is to use it as a resource in the sermon. When we use ourselves as illustrations or as a case study, we are rightfully using the self to authenticate and confirm the truth of the sermon's text. The preacher's attitude, earnestness and enthusiasm, as well as his or her expression of love and joy, can be powerful in getting the message across to the people. Veterans of the pulpit testify that the most effective illustrations come from their own experiences told not to glorify themselves but to demonstrate the power of God in their lives.

Even here a word of caution is in order. Personal experiences must be limited as salt is to a meal. If the people are subjected to little else but a string of personal stories and experiences Sunday after Sunday, they may tire and lose interest in seeking a message from God.

Another appropriate use of the self in a sermon is to be your real, true and genuine self. There is no place for a phony in the pulpit.

This phoniness can be expressed sometimes in an unnatural tone of voice or manner of speaking, sometimes called the "stained glass voice." There is a tendency among preachers to put on airs, to be someone other than the real person. This ends up appearing to be insincerity and superficiality and can be quickly perceived by the people. Artificiality turns people off.

John the Baptizer is a good example. When the Pharisees asked him who he was he refused to pose as anyone else, though it would have been a high compliment. No, he was not Elijah nor the Messiah. He was only a voice in the wilderness calling for repentance. He refused to be called the Light when he knew he was only a witness to the Light. A preacher needs to say, "I am what I am." We come to God as we are, and he will use us as we are, simple, plain, humble spokespersons for Christ.

A group of parishioners was asked to write down what they hoped to experience in a sermon. The majority answered, "A man speaking." They wanted to hear God speaking to them through a genuine human being, whether male or female.

While self cannot be separated from a sermon, a third appropriate thing to do with self is to forget self; to be aware of self can ruin a sermon. We tend to think of ourselves in the act of preaching. In our minds we may ask, "Will I find favor with the people?" "Will I offend anyone?" "Will the visitors come back next Sunday?" We become self-conscious about what and how we are preaching, especially when we see a church dignitary or a statesman such as a mayor or governor or a professional person in the congregation.

For effective preaching you must forget yourself. Become so engrossed in the subject and the issue that you can think only of the message and the hearers. This gives you tremendous freedom. Tensions and fears are lost. Throw yourself into the sermon so that the sermon is incarnated in you. Live and breathe the message, and it is second nature to you. Then the sermon becomes dynamic and the gestures are natural and spontaneous.

It has been said that when a sermon is over, the response of the people should not be, "What a great preacher!" but "What a great Christ!" Take yourself and hide behind the cross so that people will not see you but the Christ on the cross. This is possible by imitating St. Paul in his preaching, "For we do not preach ourselves, but Jesus Christ as Lord."

Chapter 13

Getting Personal in Preaching

What do people say about our sermons? We preachers feel complimented when we are told, "You spoke to me today" or "You touched me" or "I got a lot out of your sermon." On the other hand, we feel we have failed if someone asks, "What's that got to do with me?"

Do we preachers look at our sermons from our perspective or from the people's? Are we dishing out Sunday after Sunday what *we* think people ought to hear, or do we consider what *people* want to hear? If we are not preaching with them in mind, they may hear but not listen. After an analysis of two hundred sermons a Swiss homiletician, Hans Van der Geest, calls attention to the need for personal preaching.

A Personal Preacher

Personal preaching calls for the preacher to be personable. People will listen to a warm, compassionate and friendly preacher. If the preacher is cold, formal, aloof and distant, they do not get the message of the sermon. A lovely little girl always sat close to the pulpit in order to look up at the preacher who always had a smile for her. One Sunday she went home sobbing. At first her mother could not find out the reason for her crying. Finally the girl said, "I looked at God all morning and he never smiled at me once!"

A personable preacher is one who is likable and outgoing. People want a preacher who is genuine, sincere and earnest. They will usually not listen to one whom they sense does not truly believe what he or she is preaching.

How does a preacher become personable? We can begin by bringing to life the Word we preach. We need to put ourselves into the message and get involved in what we are saying so that the message can be felt as well as heard. This calls for preaching filled with enthusiasm, earnestness and vitality. When the sermon is clothed with the enthusiasm and excitement of the preacher, it becomes a living thing. The message can come alive through animated gestures, facial expressions and the voice's tone and volume.

Moreover, the sermon can be made personal by *occasionally* sharing one's own experiences without calling attention to or bringing credit to oneself. Sharing doubts, failures or problems enables the people to see that the preacher is also human. Then there is the matter of language. Are we speaking in the people's tongue? The miracle of Pentecost was the Spirit's enabling of the apostles to speak in the languages of people from various countries. Today we ought to be less interested in "speaking in tongues" and more concerned about speaking in the tongue of the common people. This demands that we do not speak Elizabethan English but the language of the person on the street, without stooping to crude slang or ecclesiastical jargon which demands a glossary for understanding.

Personal preaching comes about also by not referring excessively to a manuscript or notes in the pulpit. You need constant eye contact to convey to people that you are talking to them personally. How do you feel when a person does not look at you when he or she speaks to you? When we preach, do we talk *at* or *with* people? A pastor who constantly refers to notes breaks that eye contact. To preach without total dependence on notes takes hard work, thorough preparation and saturation with the subject, plus a logical and simple outline. But the reward is truly personal communication with our people.

The People's Desire

We have looked at the need for the preacher to be personable. Now we want to look at personal preaching from the people's viewpoint.

People want from preaching a feeling of warmth, uplift and encouragement. One woman went from church to church and explained, "I am trying to find a place where someone speaks to my needs." People usually do not consider theological ideas, doctrines or concepts of first importance. Some preachers look at sermons from a seminarian's viewpoint. We can focus too much on the biblical languages, technical exegesis, dry doctrines, deep philosophical insights, logic and clear outlines.

But this is not what makes people listen to sermons. They want to leave church feeling they have been spiritually touched and inspired. Once I heard a sermon which from a homiletical viewpoint was a failure. But afterwards I heard a worshiper say to the pastor, "That was a wonderful sermon." Regardless of how many homiletical principles were violated, this man received a blessing from the sermon. He went home uplifted and strengthened. How can we account for it? It spite of the sermon's technical problems, the man's heart was warmed. He was helped. He represents most people who are longing for warmth and inspiration. The sermon he heard conveyed to him compassion and stirred up hope.

This emphasis on "creating good feelings" has some dangers in it. We preachers may think that it does not matter *what* we preach as long as we convey encouragement and hope. If we touch people's hearts, the content or the form of the sermon does not matter. But it would be disastrous to fall into that trap. Content *is* important. Form is necessary to convey the truth of God in Christ.

The other danger is that we may be tempted to manipulate people's emotions. We can fall prey to sentimentalism. We may (God forbid!) turn to tear-jerking illustrations designed only for emotional response. Our task is to preach the truth in such a way that it is heartwarming. Our challenge each Sunday is to touch the heart, feed the mind and move the will.

Chapter 14

Take Time to Read

"Reading makes a full man," said John Wesley. If that is true, it explains why we preachers are often empty and our sermons are shallow. It is a tragedy when the preacher *has* to say something on Sunday morning but really has nothing to say.

A hearing-impaired man and his friend were seated on the front pew. As the sermon progressed, he kept asking his friend, "What did he say? What did he say?" Finally in exasperation the friend whispered loudly for many to hear, "Keep quiet! I told you I'd tell you if he says anything!"

Only preachers know what a task and challenge it is to preach to the *same* congregation Sunday after Sunday, year after year. The preacher faces the demand to say something new, to have a new idea or new approach at least fifty times a year. This is equivalent to writing a book each year. The average sermon has ten thousand to twelve thousand words. In a year that amounts to 600,000 words. Who can measure up to this task?

The problem is exacerbated by the fact that the lectionary gives us the same lessons year after year on a three-year cycle for each Sunday. In Series B, for instance, we are to preach for five Sundays on John chapter six. We got through it one year, but can we do it with freshness when it comes up again? Moreover, we preach a gospel which does not change. Add to this, most of our people have heard passages of Scripture over and over through the years. What can we say that we have not already said? It is not a matter of creating new wine, for the gospel ever remains the same. But we must find new wineskins in which to hold God's Word. We can become desperate for a new approach, a new insight, a different idea.

Reading is one solution to this problem. Is it possible that within a year a preacher does not read one book other than the Bible? A Protestant bishop confessed to me that because of administrative duties and preaching ordination, anniversary and dedication sermons Sunday after Sunday, he had not read a book for some years. A parish pastor can be as busy as a bishop with meetings, counseling, calls and home responsibilities. Practically every pastor would think that he or she was in heaven if there were time to read a book. Indeed, we pastors do read. We have newspapers, magazines and more than enough promotional material from denominational headquarters. But to read a good, solid book is another matter!

Time to Read

As a parish pastor for twenty-eight years, I faced this problem, so I can write out of personal experience. To keep from becoming shallow, to keep from repeating myself, I found that I had to find and take time to read. This was true whether I had a congregation of a hundred or a thousand. John Wesley advised his pastors: "Read at least five hours of every twenty-four; otherwise you will be a trifler all your days, and a pretty superficial preacher."

First, you must ask if you are making the best use of your time. How much time are you giving to television? Would some of that time be better spent with a book? Are you giving too much time to the daily newspaper or a weekly news magazine? When I was a student in seminary, Paul Scherer told us in a special lecture always to read the daily newspaper standing up to avoid spending too much time with trivia. Are we preachers spending too much time after meetings indulging in small talk when we might be reading in our studies?

How can a busy pastor find time to read and not neglect pastoral duties? One possibility is to read a solid book little by little in connection with one's daily personal devotions. Few pastors can read a book from cover to cover in a day or two. It is the genius who can read a book a day. Parish responsibilities will not permit it. E. Stanley Jones taught me a valuable lesson when he recommended reading fifty to sixty pages each day. I find that I can read several weighty books per year by reading one chapter a day as enrichment during the daily hour set aside for devotions.

One pastor takes several weeks each year during the summer for reading. He does a minimal amount of parish work and spends the rest of the time at home with his books. Other pastors take an armful of books with them on their annual month's vacation. This, however, can get you into trouble with your family. Since there is so much to read to keep up with the church and world, one should never be without reading material during the day. Time after time a pastor must wait—for a meeting to start, for a counselee to appear, for a hospital patient made ready to receive visitors, for a plane to take off. Why waste precious time when there is so much to read?

A pastor is justified in taking this time for in reading he or she is getting ideas, facts, insights and illustrations that will make this Sunday's sermon worth the people's time. Have you ever stopped to calculate how much time your congregation is giving to the sermon? Each Sunday worshipers give an hour on the average to come and go and another hour for the service. If there are two hundred people present, you are given four hundred hours of their time. Is it not reasonable, then, to take time to read so that the sermon will be worth their time? It is a tragedy when someone leaves church on Sunday and feels that it was not worth his time and effort to have come.

What to Read

In the course of a year as a guest preacher or teacher I see many pastors' studies and their libraries. I never fail to look for a book I may want to read some day. In many libraries the books were bought when the pastor was in seminary. Most books are outdated and outmoded. This says something about the pastor's reading habits. If the library holds recent books they usually deal with the practice of ministry: counseling, administration, publicity, marriage, promotion and books of sermons. They might be classified as "how-to" books—to be read once for sermon illustrations, then to collect dust and create moving expenses for the next appointment or call.

In this day of expensive books this is a wise rule to follow in buying volumes for your library: Do not buy a book you will read only once, but buy reference books to which you will go repeatedly year after year. The one-time books may be borrowed from a public or seminary library.

For the average parish pastor, there is a problem of knowing what books to read. Pastors often ask me, "What was the best book you read within the past year?" When one gets away from the lists of recommended books handed out by professors and gets involved in sixteen-hour-per-day parish work, the average pastor gets away from the world of academia. The advertisements in church periodicals give us titles and authors of recent books, but we do not know which ones are worth our time and money. Book reviews are helpful, especially those in *Christian Century, Interpretation* and *Theology Today.*

For maximum benefit you need to read the heavy, meaty books. They are not easy reading. You may have to read a paragraph twice before you get the thought clearly in mind. But it is like chewing solid meat. It is nourishing, provocative and enlightening. You may not get sermon illustrations or quotations, but your mind will be stretched. New insights will be gained. This gives you grist for your homiletical mill. These books will stimulate you to give something fresh on Sundays.

There is light reading too. Newspapers and news magazines are interesting and at the same time keep us up-to-date with the world. There are church periodicals that keep us abreast of the church. Biographies and historical novels can be helpful in securing illustrative material. At the end of a hard day you may need something light to help you relax before going to bed. Paperback novels are good for that: mystery, romance, western.

Whether seeking enlightenment or relaxation, for a preacher the admonition is "Read, read, read!"

Part III

The Message of Preaching

I hear the sermon, but who is speaking? The preacher? Not so. You do not hear the preacher. The voice, to be sure, is his, but my God speaks the Word which the preacher speaks.

—Martin Luther

* * * * *

The medium becomes the message only if the messenger has nothing to say.

—John W. Bachman

Chapter 15

A Theology of Preaching

What is preaching all about? What are you doing when you are preaching? Who is speaking, you or God? Can anyone preach? Can a lay person really preach? If so, what is the meaning of being called or ordained to preach? Is there any difference between an address and a sermon?

These questions and others that can be raised are answered through developing a theology of preaching. Before anyone undertakes the task of preaching, he or she should work out a theology of preaching. What a preacher says depends largely upon his or her understanding of the preaching task.

There is a world of difference between an address and a sermon. What some call a sermon is nothing more than an address. A sermon is a unique form of public speaking, unlike any other type of public address. Sermons and addresses can be contrasted in many ways.

Horizontal/Vertical Dimensions

A public speech (address, lecture, etc.) involves a horizontal dimension in communication. One person (the speaker) talks to another person (the listener). They are conversing on a level plane, communicating between equals. The speaker is telling a group of people what he or she thinks, believes and suggests. It is person to person communication.

A sermon is the opposite of an address. It contains the vertical dimension—God speaking through a person to others. A sermon involves preaching.

In an address there may be speech *about* God. As such, the address can be educational, interesting and helpful, but it still boils down to the act of one person telling others his or her ideas about God.

But in a sermon God speaks. A recent cartoon showed a small boy with his family in church listening to a sermon. In a loud whisper the boy asked his mother while pointing to the pulpit, "Is that God up there?" Dr. William Holmes Borders of Atlanta says occasionally during a sermon, "Now I am the voice of God."

Dr. Borders understands the biblical meaning of a sermon. It is claimed that the prophets said more than fifteen hundred times, "Thus saith the Lord." The meaning of "prophet" is "one who speaks for another." The "another" is God. Jeremiah was convinced that he was the voice of God: "The Lord sent me to prophesy against this house and this city all the words you have heard. Now therefore amend your ways and your doings, and obey the voice of the Lord your God. . . . For in truth the Lord sent me to you to speak all these words in your ears" (Jeremiah 26:1-15, author's paraphrase).

In the New Testament, the common word for preaching is *kerussein*. From this word comes *kerux*, meaning "herald." One who preaches is a herald. A herald never speaks for himself but says only what he is commanded to say to the people.

Does this view mean that everything that is said from the pulpit is the Word of God? The apostle Paul did not think so, for he distinguished between God's words and his own. In 1 Corinthians 7:25 Paul wrote: "Now about virgins: I have no command from the Lord, but I give a judgment as one who by the Lord's mercy is trustworthy." Paul distinguished his personal opinions from his preaching.

Also, we realize that the pulpit sometimes contains false prophets who have always plagued God's people. Listen to the complaint of Ezekiel: "And her prophets have daubed for them with whitewash, seeing false visions and divining lies for them, saying, 'Thus says the Lord God' when the Lord has not spoken" (Ezekiel 13:6, author's paraphrase).

When, then, during a sermon is it God or the preacher speaking, and when is the speaking a sermon or an address? Diligent prayer and study will help the preacher separate his or her own views and opinions from the true Word of the Lord. In spite of ourselves we can allow prejudices to creep into our sermons. For example, look at a sermon you preached ten years ago and you may be surprised at what you said then. Today you might not preach the same sermon.

Sacrificial/Sacramental Elements

An address can deal with a religious subject on which the speaker gives his or her insights, telling all he or she knows about and has experienced with God. He or she can talk about how good God has been and how Christ changed his or her life. This is a witness to the congregation. Such an address can be stimulating and informative. It may be appreciated by the people. As such it can be considered a sacrificial element of worship, that which is offered to God in praise and thanksgiving. But no matter how fine and interesting this address may be, it is still only an address. It is one person speaking *about* God. It is not a sermon.

A sermon is a sacramental act of worship. A sacrament is a means of grace coming from God and accepted by a person in faith. It is the means by which God's love and truth come to people. A sacrament is the Word of God coming to us in oral (sermon), visible (sacrament) and written (Bible) forms. The sermon is the sacramental proclamation of the Word of God. Luther said, "Preaching is the Word of God."

The apostle Paul related preaching to faith and salvation. Through the proclamation of the gospel people gain knowledge of Christ and gain faith to respond to God. Preaching creates and nurtures faith. In Romans 10 Paul said, "So faith comes from what is heard, and what is heard comes by the preaching of Christ" (RSV). Preaching is a part of God's plan of salvation. Through preaching God calls people to believe in Christ as Lord and Savior. It is not preaching as a method that convicts and convinces people, but it is the Word that is preached.

This makes preaching a sacramental act of worship. In and through the sermon God is calling, convicting, comforting and challenging his people. God is busy during a sermon, and he is using his preacher as an instrument to accomplish his purpose of serving his people. A sermon, then, is something that God does; it is a means of grace. A sermon is a Word-event. God acts while the sermon is being preached. And the preacher serves only as a midwife to the birth of new babes in Christ.

Ego/Christ-Centered

In an address the central figure is the speaker, the "I," who speaks for himself or herself. The person tells of his or her ideas and is the authority for what is spoken. When he or she gets through, listeners may say, "What a good speaker" or "What a learned man" or "What a personality!" The speaker gets all the credit and glory for what was said.

But a true sermon is Christ-centered. The preacher as a person hides behind the cross so that he or she will not be seen. The ambition is to speak so that the people will not hear him or her but Jesus only. Paul wrote, "We preach Christ crucified" (1 Corinthians 1:23). We have been ordained to "preach the Word," and the Word is Jesus Christ, the incarnate Word of God, full of grace and truth. Jesus is the full and final revelation of God. To preach less than Christ means not giving the whole truth.

The presence of Christ in the sermon is proof that it is a Christian sermon. A message dealing only with social problems or personal ethics without Christ is merely an address. A Christian sermon presents and exalts Jesus Christ as the way, truth and life. Christ-centered preaching calls for preaching the gospel, the life, death and resurrection of Christ. In each sermon there must be enough of the gospel that a non-Christian would hear the answer to the question, "What must I do to be saved?"

For a sermon to be Christ-centered it must do more than merely mention the name of Jesus, quote his words or use him as a mere example. Just extolling Jesus as a teacher, prophet or man of great integrity does not make a Christ-centered sermon. It is only when Jesus is preached as Lord and Savior that the sermon is Christ-centered.

Opinion/Truth

A sermon is also different from an address in that an address primarily consists of the speaker's opinions. What he or she says is an opinion of the truth gained from reading, study, experience and/or consultation with others.

People in the pews often think of a sermon in terms of an address, as a human speaking. When the sermon is discussed and someone says, "That's just your opinion," the implication is that his or her opinion is as valid as the preacher's. If the sermon of the day is only an address, the layperson is entitled to say, "But that's just your opinion; I have mine, too." If a listener sees the sermon only as a sharing of opinions, the sermon has lost its authority and power.

However, if the sermon is Christ-centered, it will not consist only of the preacher's opinion but of the truth. For Christ is the truth of God. He is the truth made flesh. His words are truth because he is the mouth of God; this truth is not one of many truths, but he is the final truth. Christ's truth is not about politics, social organization, economics or science; it is spiritual truth dealing with the truth about God, humanity, sin and salvation. It is the gospel truth about life. If a sermon is God speaking, then his word is truth. This gives a sermon a sense of certainty, and the preacher can present the sermon with confidence because he or she knows it is not personal opinion but the very truth of God. It is this sense of certainty that is missing when a sermon is only an address.

Research/Revelation

The content of a public speech, whether it is a lecture or an address, comes primarily from the speaker's research. Having consulted the authoritative books written by human beings, he or she gathers the material, organizes it and puts it in a form for public presentation.

What a sermon has to say does not come from research only but also includes revelation. Paul makes that clear: "The gospel I preached is not something that man made up. I did not receive it from any man, nor was I taught it; rather, I received it by revelation from Jesus Christ" (Galatians 1:11-12). In 1 Corinthians 15 Paul again emphasizes that the gospel he preached was "what I also received." The truth of the gospel is too great and too profound for any human mind to have manufactured it. It has to be given from above. The truth of God is not invented but given by revelation. God disclosed himself through the ages, through history and finally in Christ. This is the truth that we have inherited, the treasure now presented in earthen vessels. The gospel is the rich heritage of the church, its true treasure. It is for us preachers today to know that revelation, to embrace it until it is our very own gospel and then to share it through preaching.

Where is this revelation found? It takes us back once again to the Bible as the record of God's revelation through history. That is why revelation is absolutely indispensable for preaching. Though the phrase, "The Bible says," may be abused, there is truth in it. "Jesus loves me. This I know, for the Bible tells me so." Christ died for our sins—that is true because the Bible says so. The truth of a sermon is nothing new; it is not the creation of the preacher's mind. It is the same truth preached by the apostles and the reformers. It is the preacher's task today to take the "old, old story of Jesus and his love" and to put it in today's language and thought forms that are meaningful to people of this generation.

Experimentation/Experience

When an address is given the speaker may use experimentation to get to the message. This is the scientific method of our age. We gather material. We experiment to see if the hypothesis is valid. After the experimentation we come to some conclusions which are valid until further experimentation proves the previous conclusion is no longer tenable.

The truth of a sermon is not the result of experimentation. The sermon testifies to the truth of the sermon by virtue of experience. It may not always be the experience of the preacher, but it may be the experience of others either in the Bible or in church history. Paul could say, "I know whom I have believed." That was experience. The truth of God is validated by one's own experience. It is not dependent upon experimentation. It has already happened to me and in my life. For example, here is a truth: God is good. This can be claimed as true because of the experience of God's goodness in one's life.

One of the secrets of great preaching is that the pulpit giants of the church in every generation without exception have had a real experience with God in Christ. This experience has confirmed God's truth and has given the preacher a sense of assurance and confidence in his proclamation.

Discussion/Proclamation

When an address is over it is often open for discussion. Questions are raised and opposing opinions may be given. The speaker and hearer enter into a dialogue on the content of the address. It is discussed in the hope that further truth might come forth. The speaker gives his or her opinion, and now others may share their opinions on the subject. Through this dialogue it is hoped that all might come closer to the truth.

But a sermon does not exist merely to provoke discussion. A sermon is *kerygma,* a proclamation of the truth received by revelation. The preacher tells what God has done in history, especially in the Christ-event. "This is what God has done for us!" It is like a newscast on radio or television. The announcer should make sure that he or she does not comment on the news. The purpose is just to tell what happened in the world, nation or city. This is what a preacher should do with the sermon. He or she tells the people about the facts of the gospel. "This is what God has done." "This happened on the cross and at Joseph's tomb." Because of the preacher's love and concern for mankind, he or she appeals to people to accept the facts proclaimed.

Symptoms/Solution

An address given by a speaker usually deals with symptoms of the world's condition. The address deals with a diagnosis of our disease. It tells us what is wrong with society. It describes conditions—injustice, discrimination, poverty and misery. These are symptoms of our problems, our sickness. If a solution is suggested, it is just the speaker's answer to the problem. It is open to questioning and discussion. Not all would agree with the speaker's solution. In an address, questions upon questions are raised, but often no answers are available or the answer given is not generally acceptable. When the address is over, we are no better off except that we may understand our predicament a little better.

Some feel the same about a sermon. They claim that a sermon exists to pose only questions. Answers, they say, do not belong in the pulpit. If that is true, then a sermon is not a sermon; it is only an address by a person.

But a sermon is God's Word, presenting God's truth, and God has the answer to the human problem. He is the solution to man's illness. If a sermon does not have a solution or answer, it is a waste of people's time. We are then offering them a stone instead of bread. The hungry sheep go home dissatisfied and unfilled. Tragically this is too often the case in today's churches.

The solution to humanity's condition is Jesus Christ. The basic answer is still Christ. "Christ is the answer" may be an overused phrase, but the truth is still valid. This is because our problems—whether economic, social, national or international—are basically moral and spiritual problems. Crime, war and greed in business are moral problems. Morality is the fruit of religion, and religion deals with a person's relationship with God. The saying is still true: We will not get the world straightened out until humanity is straightened out. There is only one way to straighten out a person: repentance and faith in Christ.

This focus on Christ gives a sense of urgency and importance to preaching. Here is the solution, O earth! In Christ we have the answer to your questions, the solution to your problems. Here is the good news for modern man!

Reformation/Redemption

An address may deal with the immoral condition of the times and call for moral improvement. This can be a moral pep talk, an ethical treatise and an emotional appeal to do better. An address can point out the horrors of social injustice and decry the effects of the underworld. An address may call for reformation of persons and society.

In this age of scandals we cannot deny the need for calls to a higher ethical code. But to limit our preaching to this is to put band-aids on our social sores and personal hurts. A sermon differs from an address because it is not satisfied only with the reformation of society but calls also for the redemption of society. Christianity is a religion of redemption, with the Cross at its very heart. People do not need to be reformed; they need to be remade. This inner renewal comes only when people are born again of the Holy Spirit. We must call for conversion based upon genuine repentance and true faith in Christ as Savior.

A sermon calls sinners to repentance. It points to Christ as the solution to the problem of sin, both personal and social. Indeed, a reformed way of life will follow redemption as surely as fruit comes from the vine.

Conclusions/Commitment

When an address is given, usually some conclusion is drawn containing some aspect of truth on the subject discussed. The listener may accept it or reject it. The matter ends there. The address may have been entertaining and/or educational or a waste of time. The speaker is not necessarily concerned whether listeners buy the conclusion or not. He or she walks away from the speech and it is all over.

But a sermon calls for commitment. Its purpose is not only to give the truth, but also to bring the listener to a commitment based on the truth proclaimed. A sermon does not deal primarily with an idea to be embraced but a person to be loved, followed and obeyed. John's gospel puts it this way: "These are written that you may believe that Jesus is the Christ, the Son of God, and that by believing you may have life in his name" (John 20:31).

A sermon is different from an address in that it calls for a decision. The preacher calls out for a verdict. The purpose of the sermon is to persuade people to follow Christ and make a total commitment to him. This is what every true sermon aims to do: bring people to a new or renewed relationship with God by faith in Jesus Christ.

Chapter 16

The Sacrament of Preaching

The true treasure of the church consists of the Word and the sacraments. Ministers are ordained to preach the Word and administer the sacraments, which for Protestants are baptism and the Lord's Supper (Holy Communion, Eucharist). We usually refer to the Word and sacraments as though they were two different realities. In fact, the three (Word, baptism, Holy Communion) are one. Basically there is but one sacrament, the Word.

There is one sacrament because of the nature of the Word and sacraments. What is the Word? It is the revelation of God's truth and grace perfectly and ultimately expressed in Jesus Christ. The Bible bears witness to this self-revelation of God. To preach the Word, either from the Old or New Testament, is to preach Christ crucified and risen.

What is a sacrament? It is the Word of God accompanied by a visible sign, water or bread and wine. A sacrament is basically and essentially the Word of God which comes to us as a means of grace to bless, forgive and transform us.

Thus the Word comes to us in a threefold manner. The Word comes in a written form, the Bible. It also comes in an oral form, preaching. The third mode for the Word is the Eucharist. All three modes are equally important and efficacious. One means of grace is not superior to the others. A mature Christian needs and takes advantage of all three.

The Oral Word of God

What is preaching? It is the oral form of the Word of God. St. Augustine said, "Preaching is an audible sacrament." Luther called the church a "mouth house" and defined preaching as a mouth affair. The Second Helvetic Confession says, "The preaching of the Word of God is the Word of God." If preaching is the Word of God, then a sermon is a sacrament. The sermon as a sacrament makes biblical preaching a necessity and a correct exegesis of the text a must. A sermon is not the Word of God if it consists merely of the preacher's opinions of the text, but rather the Word in the text must be heard for the sermon to be qualified as the Word of God.

How then is a biblical sermon the Word of God, the means of grace? Through preaching a listener is confronted with Christ, for "we preach Christ crucified" (1 Corinthians 1:23). People look to the pulpit saying, "Sir, we would like to see Jesus" (John 12:21).

Faith in Christ comes out of this preaching: "Consequently, faith comes from hearing the message, and the message is heard through the word of Christ" (Romans 10:17). Salvation is a product of grace, and grace is received by faith. If faith comes from preaching, then the sermon is an act of salvation, a means of grace, a sacrament.

Furthermore, the Spirit is received during the hearing of the Word. For example, Peter preached to Cornelius and his company (Acts 10:44). The Holy Spirit came to those listening to his sermon, because Word and Spirit are inseparable. The Spirit comes with the Word causing people to confess Christ as Lord: "No one cay say 'Jesus is Lord,' except by the Holy Spirit" (1 Corinthians 12:3).

Through the preached Word the Holy Spirit calls a person to believe in Christ and to join the community of faith. The result is salvation (forgiveness, acceptance) through the preached Word. Thus a sermon is God's act of calling, accepting and forgiving a sinner. Since salvation is a process, this sacramental work of God in the preached Word applies to both saints and sinners.

Weekly Communion?

All this is said as background in order to object to the current trend in Protestant churches to insist upon a weekly administration of Holy Communion as the climax and epitome of worship. The revised liturgies now appearing insist that worship is not complete unless the Sacrament of the Altar is celebrated. For example, in the new *Lutheran Book of Worship* the name of the chief worship service was changed from "The Service" to "Holy Communion," indicating that each Sunday the Communion should be administered.

In some cases, the Holy Communion even eliminates the sermon. For example, at the dedication of the new three-million-dollar chapel at Emory University a few years ago, there was no sermon. In its place, representatives of the student body, faculty and administration gave brief remarks and the Eucharist was celebrated.

Weekly Communion has certain disadvantages. This is not to minimize the Holy Communion or to suggest that this sacrament should not be offered to the people. It should be administered in obedience to Jesus' command, "Do this in remembrance of me." But he did not say it should be done daily or weekly. A monthly Communion seems reasonable. It could also be available each Sunday at an early service or between morning services or at the close of a preaching service. For example, to keep the worship service within an hour, we rush through the service under the pressure of time, omit the confession of sin, limit the sermon to a few minutes and hurry the people to and from the altar rail. As a result the specialness of the Communion can be lost in the "hurry, hurry" character of the service.

Also, weekly Communion tends to become a routine affair to the point that it becomes meaningless. It happens with the constant repetition of the Lord's Prayer, the Creed and the Canticles in the liturgy. We say or sing the words mechanically without thinking of what we are saying. But, the Holy Communion is something very special, calling for special preparation in terms of confession and repentance. It is the Word coming to us in a tactile and concrete way for a mystical union with Christ and confirmation of the "remission of sins," for which Christ instituted the Supper. It should be the reenactment of a supper with Jesus, having intimate fellowship with him and sharing a meal of his own dear self given to us for our salvation.

Pastors who resist holding a weekly Communion service as the main service of the day need not feel guilty even through ecclesiastical and liturgical authorities recommend and insist upon weekly Communion. The service of the preached Word is as important as a means of grace as the administered Word in the Eucharist.

As a sacrament the preached Word is a saving Word. It can be as efficacious as the administered Word connected with bread and wine. The Word dynamically proclaimed can bring forgiveness and peace to open, repentant and believing hearts.

Biblical Preaching

Biblical preaching—is there any other kind of preaching for a Christian minister? As ordained ministers we really have no choice but to be biblical preachers! At ordination we were authorized to preach the Word: "Take authority to preach the Word." And if we are true to our own word, we must be biblical preachers for we promised at our ordination to "preach and teach the Word of God." Moreover the Bible commands ministers: "Preach the Word" (2 Timothy 4:2). Obedience requires us to be biblical preachers.

But even with your authority, promises and commands, are you a biblical preacher? You may think you are but maybe you are not. I am ashamed to confess that in the first seven years of my ministry I was not a biblical preacher. I was a topical preacher speaking on my pet subjects from Sunday to Sunday. When World War II ended I asked myself, "Now that the war is over, what am I going to preach about?" The bottom dropped out of my preaching barrel. Then I decided to take a look at the assigned lessons in the lectionary for the coming Sunday to see if I could find a sermon there. That decision was the salvation of my preaching ministry.

What Biblical Preaching Is Not

Perhaps we can see what biblical preaching is by looking at some false views of biblical preaching.

Biblical preaching is *not* using the Bible solely as a resource in terms of quotations and illustrations. This often means using the Bible to support one's own ideas. Rather, biblical preaching uses the Bible both as a source and a resource.

Biblical preaching is *not* speaking on a subject that is merely in harmony with the Bible. It may be a sermon on faith or love or hope. No one can find fault with these subjects, but the sermons on these subjects may be based on the preacher's ideas and experiences rather than on what the Bible says about them.

Biblical preaching is *not* an academic study of a passage of Scripture, providing an exegesis of the passage, explaining variant texts, possible authors, relationship to parallel passages, etc. While a good biblical sermon should contain some of this information, exegesis should not be the sole aim and purpose of the sermon.

Biblical preaching is *not* solely a lecture on the background of the text explaining biblical times and customs, history and geography. A sermon must be more than a lesson in antiquity. A biblical sermon takes the truth of an ancient text and makes it live today for the edification of the congregation.

Biblical preaching is *not* a speech about the Bible. Indeed, the Bible is the world's greatest book and is worthy of highest commendation. But a biblical sermon does not only extol the literature or wisdom of the Bible. Rather, in a biblical sermon the Bible is allowed to speak through the proclamation of the text of the sermon.

Biblical preaching is *not* just a running commentary, verse by verse, of a passage. So-called "radio preachers" often do this, failing to relate one verse to another or discuss the overall theme of the passage. A biblical sermon may use a long passage of Scripture, but the emphasis is on the theme and its main divisions.

What Biblical Preaching Is

Biblical preaching is preaching the Word of God. God's Word consists of law and gospel, which reflect the primary attributes of God—justice and love, in harmony with Jesus as Lord (law) and Savior (love). From law and gospel come judgment and salvation. A biblical preacher proclaims the Word as both law and gospel. It is said of John Newton that he preached to break a hard heart (law) and to heal a broken heart (gospel).

The challenging task of a biblical preacher is to distinguish between law and gospel and to present them in proper balance. One who preaches only the law is not a biblical preacher. A sermon on law alone results in negativism, legalism, pietism and condemnation. Such a sermon degenerates into a moral pep talk. Preachers of only the law urge people to be and do better, to try harder, to shape up. The emphasis is on words like "ought," "should" or "must." In this kind of sermon there is no gospel, no explanation of how to live the Christian life. As a result, law-only sermons produce nervous saints filled with fear and despair.

Likewise, preaching gospel without the law is not preaching the Word. The gospel is not a "must" but a "because." Because God loves, because Christ died for you—you do such and such. But the gospel alone is insufficient. To proclaim only the love of God in Christ suggests a Christianity without a cross, a cheap grace that results in sentimentalism and permissiveness. Preaching the gospel by itself results in heresies such as pluralism and universalism. The law along with the gospel is needed to convict us of our sin and show us our need of a Savior. The law is necessary while we hear the gospel so that we shall repent, for "the wages of sin is death."

Biblical preaching is preaching Jesus Christ. He is the incarnate Word. A sermon without Christ cannot be considered a biblical sermon. If we are to preach the Word, we must preach Christ, for in him "the Word became flesh." Charles Haddon Spurgeon said,

> I have heard of ministers who can preach a sermon without mentioning the name of Jesus from beginning to end. If you ever hear a sermon of that

kind, mind that you never hear another from that man. If a baker once made loaf of bread without any flour in it, I would take good care that he should never do it again, and I say the same of a man who can preach a Christ-less gospel (*Pulpit Digest*, November 1987).

Referring to Christ only as a teacher, prophet or healer is not preaching Christ. Biblical preaching proclaims Christ 1) as the way—the way to getting right with God through the redemption gained on the cross; 2) as the truth—the whole truth and nothing but the truth about God, the final and perfect revelation of God and his will; 3) as the life—life that is life in God, a life of quality that has no end.

Biblical preaching is preaching the Bible. We preach the Bible because it is the Word of God. The Bible records God's Word. The Protestant church holds to the view that the Bible as the Word of God is the sole authority in matters of faith and life. In *Theology Today* (July 1988), Mark I. Wallace writes, "In our period, the Bible is no longer regarded as a single stable book with a central message. Rather, it is a complicated text or intertext with no unifying center." This contemporary view of the Bible held by some may explain the reason for the lack of biblical preaching in our day. In contrast to this view, the traditional view held by the church is that the Bible is not a Word *about* God but *is* the Word of God. God speaks to us in and through the Word, the Bible.

The Text in Preaching

To be a biblical preacher is to preach the Bible. Obviously, no one can preach the whole Bible in one sermon. Consequently it must be done little by little. That "little" is what we mean by a text. It is a portion of Scripture used as the source of the sermon's message. A text is indispensable for biblical preaching. The word "text" comes from *texere*, meaning to weave. The text weaves the fabric of the sermon. It is as necessary as the thread used to produce a garment. The text is essential for a biblical sermon because it provides the theme and main points of the sermon.

Consider the possible uses of a text. First there is the *non-use* of a text. In *Preaching as Theology and Art* (p. 91), Elizabeth Achtemeier comments,

> It is always distressing to find a general treatment of a topic or a theological subject for which no Scripture lesson is cited. The lack of a text means that the preacher has followed his or her own progression of thought in the sermon—worst of all, it usually means that the preacher is preaching his or her own opinions on the subject, and those, of course, carry no authority whatsoever. Either our preaching and our theology grow out of the biblical witness or they are so much vanity and empty wind.

Second, there is the *misuse* or abuse of the text in preaching. Some use a text as a pretext; it simply stands at the top of the paper as a decoration. It is never used or referred to. Mrs. Virginia Gehr Stackel tells of her pastor-father who used to say when he heard this misuse of a text, "If the text had smallpox, the sermon would never have caught it." Others misuse a text as a springboard or a launching pad for their own ideas. Sometimes a text is used only as a resource to be quoted as a proof-text for the preacher's personal viewpoint. Or it can be abused when it is taken out of context, being made to say anything the preacher wants it to say.

A text also can be twisted to conform to the preacher's subject. One pastor began his sermon with these words: "When I came here two years ago, I shared with you that I always preached from a text and a good preacher can twist the text to meet whatever need he or she sees, and so I'll attempt to do that today as well."

Third, there is the *right* use of a text. After a text for the sermon is chosen, a preacher deals with the text in a threefold fashion:

1. **Exegesis.** A study is made of the text to determine the truth of the text. To find the truth, a preacher makes

a study of the text using commentaries, word studies, biblical languages, dictionaries, etc.

2. Hermeneutics. Now the preacher needs to interpret the text to answer the question, "What is the meaning of the truth in the text?" In interpreting the text the pastor keeps in mind principles of interpretation:

a. The text is to be taken literally except when the author meant it to be figurative.
b. The text is to be understood in light of the historical situation at the time of writing.
c. The text is to be considered within its context.
d. The text is to be compared with the total teaching of the Bible.
e. The text is to be seen and understood in light of Christ.

3. Homiletics. Now the preacher looks at the text for its applicability to life today. What difference does the text make? What are the practical implications of the text for the lives of the people?

Types of Biblical Sermons

There are at least three different ways a text can be developed which result in different types of biblical sermons. Let us look at Matthew 2:1-12 and see how three different types of sermons can come out of the same passage.

1. Thematic sermon. In this sermon the text provides the theme of the sermon. It is of utmost importance that the theme of the text, determined by the exegesis, is the theme of the sermon. The text may be short or long, just enough to provide the theme. The text is Matthew 2:2. The theme is worship. A preacher takes this theme and develops it as he or she sees fit. The outline may be:

A. The nature of worship
B. The method of worship
C. The value of worship

2. **Textual sermon.** The text is the same: Matthew 2:2. In a textual sermon the text is short, because the focus is upon the key words of the text.

Theme: Why are you here?
A. Who are we?—"We"
B. Purpose of our coming—"Worship"
C. The one we worship—"Him"

3. **Expository sermon.** Our text remains Matthew 2:1-12. For an expository sermon, the text is usually lengthy—a paragraph, chapter, or even a book of the Bible—because the focus is upon the ideas or truths of the passage.

Theme: The Wise Worship
A. Wise people seek—vv. 1-2
B. Wise people get directions—vv. 3-8
C. Wise people give gifts—vv. 10-11
D. Wise people are changed—v. 12

Values of Biblical Preaching

Does biblical preaching have an advantage over non-biblical preaching? Does it make any difference to the people whether or not the message comes from the Bible, or are they content so long as the sermon is interesting and positive? Consider the following values of preaching the Bible:

• The preacher has the joy and satisfaction of fulfilling his or her call to preach the Word.
• The Word feeds the people, for it is the Bread of Life. People flock to churches where their souls are fed.
• Preaching the Bible gives the preacher confidence and courage to preach the truth, for it is not his or her word but God's.
• Biblical preaching enables the preacher to speak with the authority of God's Word.

• The Bible provides endless subjects, ideas and characters for preaching.

• Preaching the Bible deals with the needs and problems of people today.

• Biblical preaching forces a preacher to be a student of the Bible.

• Biblical preaching is powerful preaching because of the power of God's Word.

Chapter 18

Liturgical Preaching

Today we are facing a crisis in worship as well as in preaching. There is a crisis because something is wrong. Our people are not getting out of worship what they need. Consequently, we have had a decline in church attendance and membership over the past twenty years. One denomination recently reported a two-million-member loss over the past twenty years. A symptom of this crisis is a desperate search for new ways to worship and for various gimmicks to attract people to come to church.

One of the causes of this crisis is in the fact that worship and preaching are more suitable for the nineteenth rather than the twentieth century. We have not caught up with today's world, with the cultural, educational and sociological environment around us. Perhaps what we need is not radical, experimental forms of worship but a new kind of preaching that matches today's mood and culture.

Liturgical preaching helps answer today's needs. We might look at the contrast between the non-liturgical or "free" type of preaching and the liturgical style.

Rural Preaching

The first difference between non-liturgical and liturgical preaching is that the non-liturgical type is associated with a rural society and the liturgical with today's urban society. In the nineteenth century, America was primarily a rural people. In the last few decades there has been a tremendous movement from the country to the city. According to the U.S. Census Bureau, in 1987 240,000 people left the land for the town or city. Today only two percent of the U.S. population lives on farms. By contrast, in 1820 seventy-two percent worked on farms. A minister in Missouri recently reported that his county fell in population by one-half.

In the rural society the emphasis was placed upon the individual. It was a frontier environment that called for self-reliance and independence. Non-liturgical sermons fit this environment well.

Now we have a different society. It is an urban style of life which emphasizes sophistication, culture and education. Preachers now deal with an entirely different type of person. Liturgical preaching fits into this new culture of refinement and education.

Church Preaching

The second difference between liturgical and non-liturgical preaching is that non-liturgical preaching is focused upon the world while the liturgical focuses upon the church. In non-liturgical preaching, a preacher looked at the congregation in terms of prospective believers and hoped that at each service he or she would gain decisions for Christ. Today the church is not primarily composed of prospective Christians. Probably ninety-nine percent of the worshipers on a given Sunday are already Christians. They have been baptized as infants and confirmed as youth. Over the years they have been coming to church regularly. Some time ago at the close of a service a woman explained why she did not respond to an altar call: "You know, I made my decision for Christ when I was a girl."

In today's society and church, the traditional altar call seems to be a vestigial organ of non-liturgical preaching which has outlived its usefulness. If practically all in the audience are Christians, what is the use of an altar call? Apparently it is an anachronism. Is it not embarrassing for a pastor to wait for people to come forward during the singing of the last hymn and nobody comes down? It makes a preacher feel that his or her sermon had no effect. For this reason the altar call is falling into disuse. In today's church it is not only the few non-believers present who need to come forward but also the entire congregation who should have a time for re-dedication and re-consecration to Christ. In the traditional liturgy the entire congregation responds with the singing of the offertory after the sermon. Today it is not a matter of becoming a Christian for the first time but for all church members to allow Christ to enter a deeper dimension in their lives. This calls for nurture in the faith.

Evangelical Preaching

The third difference between liturgical and non-liturgical preaching is the difference between evangelical and evangelistic. In liturgical preaching the gospel is preached Sunday by Sunday to encourage growth in faith. The non-liturgical type puts emphasis upon evangelism calling for a decision often based upon emotions. The success of non-liturgical is measured by the number of converts gained after the sermon. Since our congregations are now filled with church members, this kind of preaching seems unnecessary and beside the point.

It is not hard to understand why this non-liturgical type of preaching does not appeal to many contemporary church goers. It belongs to a former century when perhaps half of the people in church had not made decisions for Christ. At the time of the American Revolution only five to six percent of the population belonged to a church. Today approximately sixty percent are church members.

In non-liturgical preaching the sermon is conceived as a tool of evangelism, and worship is used to stimulate the people to make a decision. In contrast, the liturgical sermon is an integral part of the whole worship service. A worship service contains sacramental and sacrificial elements. In the sacramental, God speaks through Scripture, sermon, benediction and absolution. In the sacrificial, worshipers speak to God through hymns, prayers,

offering and confession. When the sermon is preached,
God is speaking through a person. Through the
sacramental acts, God speaks, blesses, saves and comforts his people.

Church-Oriented Preaching

The fourth difference in these preaching styles is that
liturgical preaching is church-oriented and non-liturgical
preaching is preacher-centered. The non-liturgical
preacher is the center of the sermon and worship service.
He or she gets an idea for a sermon, then a text for the
sermon which provides the theme of the Sunday. The
Scripture lesson comes from the passage surrounding
the text. The preacher chooses the hymns that go with
the sermon. He or she lets the choir director know what
the sermon subject is so that the anthem may be on the
same theme. The prayers will deal with the theme of the
sermon. It can easily be seen that the preacher determines the theme of the entire service. This places an
enormous responsibility on the preacher.

Liturgical preaching, on the other hand, is church-
oriented. The church provides the church year with its
seasons and festivals. The Sunday of the Easter season,
for example, may be Jubilate with the theme of "Rejoice."
The church provides a lectionary from which the sermon
text is chosen. In keeping with the theme of the Sunday,
the church provides appropriate prayers and hymns.
This takes the preacher off the hook. He or she shares
the responsibility for preaching and worship with the
whole church.

Lectionary Preaching

Liturgical preaching uses the lectionary as the usual
source of texts for sermons. The church has prepared a
lectionary for use in worship and preaching since the
ancient period. Chrysostom, Augustine, Luther and the
Wesleys used the lectionary in their ministry. With the
Vatican II revised lectionary as a model, several Protestant denominations also revised their lectionaries which
had various differences. In the interest of uniformity, the

churches prepared a Common Lectionary. As of this date, Roman Catholics, Episcopalians and Lutherans have not yet revised their lectionaries to conform to the Common Lectionary.

This twentieth-century lectionary has a three-year cycle, Series A, B and C. For each Sunday corresponding to the church year, there are three lessons: The first lesson is usually taken from the Old Testament as a lesson of promise; the second lesson is usually from the epistles of the New Testament; the third lesson (gospel) is taken mostly from Matthew (Series A), Mark (Series B) and Luke (Series C). Where appropriate, John's gospel is interspersed among the three. The gospel is the fulfillment of the promise in the first lesson. The second lesson deals with interpretation and/or application of the Word for the day.

A preacher takes a text from one or more of the lessons in the lectionary. This is not a requirement. A "free" text may be chosen according to a local need or a special occasion. For regular Sunday by Sunday preaching the lectionary is most useful in providing texts and promotes long-range planning of sermons. With the use of the lectionary, preachers can plan sermons for as long as a year in advance. Usually the lessons are chosen according to a theme appropriate to the season of the church year. This theme is carried out in the psalm, hymn and prayer of the day resulting in a unified and integrated worship service.

Benefits of Liturgical Preaching

What are some of the values of liturgical preaching? The first is very practical. You will find it to be the finest aid to preaching. You are helped in planning your sermons a whole year in advance. The Scripture lessons for each Sunday are chosen for you. You will take your text from these passages. The church provides a theme for each Sunday, and your sermon and service will be built on that theme.

Second, liturgical preaching gives balance to your preaching. If you do not use the lectionary, you have the responsibility of providing a balanced diet of spiritual food Sunday after Sunday, year after year. Not many preachers are able to do this adequately. A pastor said, "I took all my past sermons and arranged them according to the books of the Bible. I found that practically all of my sermons came from Matthew and John. The Old Testament was not considered and the rest of the New Testament was barely touched." A ministerial student reported that on Pentecost he followed the lectionary and preached on the Holy Spirit. After the service a woman told him, "You know, that's the first time in ten years I have heard a sermon on the Holy Spirit in this church." Recently the Presbyterians found in a survey that the average minister has sixty-five favorite texts that are imposed on congregations year after year.

A third benefit of liturgical preaching is that it is seasonal. There is a right and wrong time for everything, even in preaching. When is the right time to preach on the cross—in July? When does one consider the Holy Spirit? When is the right time psychologically, theologically and spiritually for a particular theme? The church year with lectionary answers these questions for you.

Then there is the value of comprehensiveness. If you use the lectionary you will preach on every major doctrine of the Bible. In the course of a year you cover the entire life and teaching of the Savior.

Liturgical preaching is also ecumenical. In a world like ours it is important for the church to give a united witness and make a united impact. It is a wonderful thought and feeling that your fellow-ministers are speaking on the same general theme on a particular Sunday. You feel you are in tune with the message of the universal church. You blend your voice with all your fellow-preachers in declaring the Word of that particular day.

To be a liturgical preacher is to be a biblical preacher. A liturgical preacher faces three biblical passages to read, study and use each Sunday. He or she knows that a text is to be taken from these passages, which calls for a study of them. In and through the sermon the people will be fed as the Bible is expounded, explained and applied to their lives.

The greatest value of all is that liturgical preaching requires Christ-centered preaching. A true liturgical preacher will say with St. Paul, "We preach not ourselves but Jesus Christ and him crucified." The church year with the lectionary revolves around the life and teachings of Jesus. The hub of the church year's wheel is Christ. The spokes of the wheel are the seasons. The circumference of the wheel consists of the fifty-two Sundays. If a preacher uses the church year with the lectionary, he or she will be led to speak on some aspect of Jesus' life and work. And this, after all, is the true test of a preacher of the Word.

In the history of preaching across twenty centuries, one of the marks of great preaching is liturgical preaching. If preaching is to regain its primary place in the church and if it is going to make its rightful impact on the world, preaching for today and tomorrow must become liturgical.

Chapter 19

Narrative Preaching

In preaching, as in other areas of life, there are fads. Just as there are new clothing fashions and new models for cars, there are trends in preaching styles. In the 1970s we had dialogue preaching, talk-back sessions and experimental preaching. I know, for I spent a sabbatical quarter experimenting with new forms of preaching with a long-suffering congregation in Clearwater, Florida.

In the 1980s the rave has been narrative or story preaching. This new emphasis in preaching seems to be a reaction to the direct, confrontive approach emphasized in the seventies. The cardinal virtue then was honesty, even to the point of being rude, crude and offensive. We were told to "let it all hang out" and to "tell it like it is."

But this bold, direct approach to preaching seems to have run its course. We have returned to the subtle, indirect approach promulgated by Kirkegaard and recently popularized by Craddock's *Overhearing the Gospel.* It is claimed that the indirect method is a more effective form of communication. A spate of new books on story preaching is coming off the presses. Today a preacher must decide if he or she will adopt this new preaching style. But before a decision is made, it may be well to learn more about the new method.

What Is Narrative Preaching?

Story or narrative preaching is described as "shared story." What is a story? It is defined as "anything in which specific characters and events influence each other to form a meaningful narrative."

Of course, there is nothing new about stories. Special programs for children are called "story hours." When we were children we pleaded, "Tell us a story!" As parents we read Bible stories to our children. A popular hymn says, "I love to tell the story . . . of Jesus and his love."

Proponents of story preaching insist that the story is the sermon, not just a part of it useful for illustration. The story stands on its own merit and needs no explanation nor application. We are told that narrative preaching involves three strands: the story, the preacher's story and the people's story. These three are to be woven together into a unified discourse. In some ways there is little that is new about this use of story, for traditional preaching has always involved these three elements: the message is the story; the preacher tells the story; the message is given to the people.

Story as a technique, proponents claim, is a more effective means of communication. People receive the message indirectly. They do not hear the gospel; they overhear it just as adults overhear the message delivered to children in the children's sermon or at a wedding when the sermon is addressed to the wedding party or at a funeral when a message is given to the bereaved but heard by friends of the family. The bold, frontal, direct approach is said to make people defensive and thus they resist the message. But story preaching slips up on the hearers and gets the message inside without the hearers realizing that they are listening to a sermon. It supposedly makes the truth more palatable.

A further advantage of story preaching is said to be that everybody loves a good story. A story captivates the attention and interest of its hearers. They get caught up in the narrative and become involved in the plot. Often people can identify with a story or with a character in it. It then becomes the individual's story.

Another appealing feature of story preaching is said to be its open-endedness. A moral does not need to be tacked on to the end. The story is to stand on its own feet. What did you think about it? What did the narrative teach? What did you get out of it?

This open-ended method appeals to some people who object to being spoon-fed with the truth or don't like being told specifically what to do and who like making up their own minds. The method appeals particularly to young people and students. The story is the message.

Is the Story the Whole Story?

Shall we buy this new wrinkle in preaching? Shall we jump on the bandwagon to be up-to-date in our preaching? Before making a decision let us consider some limitations of this style.

Does story preaching turn the preacher into a glorified or sanctified story-teller? Where will he or she find stories to tell Sunday after Sunday? To tell stories effectively each Sunday, the preacher would have to be a C.S. Lewis, a Flannery O'Connor or a Garrison Keillor. Who can measure up to those standards?

A preacher must struggle with the basic issues and needs of the day. For example, take the question, "Why does a righteous person suffer?" It is not enough for the preacher to tell a story about Job and let it end there. A preacher must wrestle with a basic human problem which he or she analyzes, studies and applies to life. Story as a vehicle is inadequate for these kinds of serious questions.

Moreover, the Bible which we preach is more than a story. Indeed, there are wonderful stories in the Bible: Creation, the Tower of Babel, the Flood, Gideon, Samson, the Exodus, David and Goliath, to mention only a few. But there also are laws in Exodus and Deuteronomy. The Psalms are not stories. There is the wisdom literature with its many precepts. The Prophets did not use the story method. The Sermon on the Mount is not a series of stories. Neither are the New Testament epistles stories. If we limit preaching to stories, much of the Bible would be out of bounds.

Preaching calls for an interpretation, explanation, illumination and application of God's truth to daily life. We preach more than a story which people are supposed to determine the meaning of and then apply to their lives. A sermon does not really begin until the rubber of the gospel hits the road of life. The sermon begins when we ask the questions, "What difference does it make?" and "What are the implications for my life today?"

In 2 Samuel 12 Nathan tells David, who has committed grievous sins, about a rich man who takes the only lamb of a very poor man for a dinner being given to a visitor. The injustice in the tale arouses David's anger, and he declares that the rich man ought to die. Then Nathan says to David, "You are that man." But Nathan does not stop there with his story. He continues with a sermon pointing out how good God has been to David and asks, "Why have you disobeyed my commands?" Judgment on David is pronounced. Then David confesses, "I have sinned against the Lord." It is not the story that convicts David of his sin, but the prophet's message from Yahweh.

Another limitation of story preaching deals with the preacher's own story. Promoters of narrative preaching insist that the preacher should tell his or her own story. But if this is done constantly, the congregation is going to tire of hearing one story after another concerning the pastor's life and experience. Story preaching can easily degenerate into subjectivism and ego-centricity. It may go against Paul's example and commitment that "We preach not ourselves," but Christ.

The gospel is more than telling a story or hearing a story about someone. A story is historical, objective, an event of the past. But Christ is more than a Galilean of the first century. He is a living reality today. Preaching must deal with the present and future as well as the past. In a sermon we hope that our listeners will be confronted with the living Christ, leading to a renewed dedication and commitment. Just telling a story is not likely to accomplish this objective.

Then there is the story itself. Is it truth or fiction? Is what we tell in a sermon-story only a myth? Who made up the story? Faith cannot be built upon fiction. When a soul's eternal destiny is at stake more than a story is needed. The message must be true to the facts and to reality in order to be believed and trusted. If we tell the gospel as a true story that actually happened, we are on the solid ground of truth. It is the only sure foundation for building a life and saving a soul.

Possible Uses of Story

Story can be used as an effective method in giving a message. However, we cannot go along with those who teach that every sermon should be a story. However, story can be used profitably in preaching.

Consider the gospel itself as story. It is a true, historical account of God's love in the life, death and resurrection of Jesus Christ. This story can be told little by little over the course of the church year by using the Common Lectionary. The church year revolves around the ministry of Jesus, from the story of his birth to the story of his ascension. Moreover, the first lectionary lesson gives the stories of the Patriarchs, Moses, David, Elijah, Elisha and the Prophets. There is ample opportunity to preach on the stories of the Old Testament.

Narrative accounts can also be used as illustrative material in a sermon. The Bible is the preacher's best source of homiletical material. Since today's generation knows little of the Bible, these stories will be fresh and appealing to most people. Since the story is used to illustrate the truth, it must necessarily be brief.

Another effective use of story is to use a Bible story as a text. Let the story provide the structure as well as the content of the sermon. Expository preaching lends itself to the use of story as a text. Imagination paints the setting of the story. The preacher puts himself or herself in the scene and identifies with it. As the story progresses, points of truth can be discussed and applied to life today.

The problem with the narrative preaching promoted today is that the whole sermon becomes nothing more than a story. There is no biblical explanation, interpretation or application to present-day living. What each listener takes from it, if anything, is what he or she wishes.

This use of story may be listed as one of the innovative types of sermons along with dialogue sermons, role playing, monologue, object lessons, etc. But from my experience with new forms of preaching, innovative kinds of preaching should not be used more often than one Sunday per month. Most worshipers prefer the traditional sermon for a regular preaching diet, but occasionally a new sermon style, such as the story form, properly used, provides variety in proclaiming the gospel.

Is There a Need for This Sermon?

In an issue of *The Christian Century*, William F. Fore tells of writing an article for *TV Guide* on the electronic church. At the time of his report, he received approximately five hundred letters in response to his article, which was critical of television ministries. In tallying up these responses he found the overall reason for people tuning into the electronic church was that the mainline churches were not meeting their needs. As one woman said, "I am trying to find a church that speaks to my needs."

This is also an accusation against contemporary preaching. If the church is to meet the needs of people, it will be done primarily through preaching. A sermon is supposed to deal with the needs of the people in the congregation. If there is no need, what is the use of preaching? It is a waste of time for the people and the preacher. Before he begins preparing the sermon a preacher should ask, "Is there a need for this sermon?" "Why am I preaching this sermon?"

An Awareness of Needs

To preach to a need, the preacher must be aware of people's needs. Without fear of exaggeration, I can say that every person in every pew is a hurting person. His or her need may not be evident nor expressed, but each person is carrying a burden. Advice columnists Ann Landers and Abigail Van Buren (Dear Abby) write for one thousand newspapers with thirteen million readers. "Dear Abby" gets twenty-five thousand letters each week. The top subjects about which people write for advice are sex, loneliness and frustration. Edgar Jackson claims that in an average congregation one-fifth of the members are mourning the loss of a loved one, one-third face marital difficulties and one-half experience difficulty adjusting emotionally to school, job, home or community.

Another basic problem of people today is a sense of emptiness. They experience an inner longing that money, fame and sex cannot fulfill. Without God people are empty. Only God can fill the vacuum in the human heart. When socialite Jean Harris was on trial for murdering diet doctor Herman Tarnhower, she confessed on the witness stand, "I wasn't sure who I was and it didn't seem to matter. I was the person in the empty chair." Many people feel that they are non-existent "nobodies."

Other basic needs of people are loneliness, guilt and a fear of death. Many people are lonely even in a crowd. They feel a loneliness for God. Many of our churches consist of singles who are lonely as they live by themselves or with their children. People also experience guilt, and they have a need for assurance of forgiveness and acceptance by God. Many people do not need to be made to feel more guilty, because they already feel guilt-stricken. But at the base of their guilt is rebellion against God, and only God can remove guilt by the power of the Cross.

Then people experience the fear of death. Though they try to push it from their minds, they have a basic fear of dying.

During World War II Helmut Thielicke was a pastor in Stuttgart. The city was ravaged by Allied bombing. One morning Thielicke stood in combat boots and military fatigues before a gaping hole which was a cellar that had suffered a direct hit the night before. Some twenty men had sought refuge there. A woman approached and

asked, "Are you Pastor Thielicke?" When he replied af-
firmatively she said, "My husband was down there last
night. All they found of him was his cap. Last Sunday we
heard you preach. I want to thank you for getting him
ready for eternity." A sermon must fulfill the fundamental
need of preparing people to face eternity.

Specific Needs

In addition to basic general needs, a preacher should
know the specific needs of his or her congregation. A
sermon needs a specific focus to deal with local needs in
the church and community. When preparing a sermon,
it is helpful to picture the people assembled for worship.
Think of the individuals and their problems. Here you see
a couple caring for their aged parents. There is a young
man with his two small daughters whose mother deserted
them last week. A young wife seated beside her husband
is considering a divorce. A man sees his wife in the choir
and is conscience-stricken by his infidelity last week.
There is a middle aged couple worried about their teen-
aged son who is taking drugs. Here is a man just laid off
from his job. Over here is an elderly woman suffering from
a terminal illness. Each person seems to have a problem,
a hurt. With longing faces they look to the pulpit for some
word of hope, comfort and guidance.

The need for the sermon should also be relevant.
There are many needs, but the needs may not apply to
the people addressed by the sermon. The need the sermon addresses should be a current and crying need.

If the needs are there and the preacher is aware of
them, then the sermon should answer the general or
specific need through the Word. People are looking to the
pulpit for answers to their problems. The answer they
hear may not be easy. But neither should the answer be
over-simplified, such as, "Believe in God and your
troubles will disappear" or "Accept Christ and you'll be a
success."

The need addressed by the sermon is so important
that during sermon preparation it should be written out

before tackling an outline for the sermon. The text must relate to this need. Does the text speak to this particular need? If not, then another text must be chosen. Moreover, the need of the sermon is inseparably related to its objective. When the need is expressed on paper, then the objective which fulfills the need can be written. When the need, text and objective are interrelated, then the outline of the sermon can be written giving the steps by which the objective will be reached and the need met.

Before you begin your next sermon, ask yourself, "Is there a need for this sermon?" If there is no need for the sermon, there is no need to prepare the sermon. When a sermon deals with a specific need in the lives of the assembled people, the sermon comes alive and speaks directly to hurting persons.

Part IV

The Methods of Preaching

When Yogi Berra was manager of a baseball team, one of the players said, "Yogi knows more about baseball than all the team put together. It's too bad he doesn't know how to tell us about it."

—Bruce Larson

Chapter 21

How to Prepare a Sermon

The story is told of a Roman Catholic priest and a rabbi who were playing golf. At one hole both had a difficult putt to make. The priest made the sign of the cross on his chest and the putt dropped into the hole. Impressed, the rabbi asked the priest if it was all right to cross himself. The priest replied, "Sure, but it won't do you any good." "Why not?" asked the rabbi. The priest explained, "Because you can't putt."

If one does not know how to preach, all of the religious observances and practices will do no good. Preaching is an art that must be learned. Preparing a sermon is a highly skilled craft. Each sermon should be a work of art. Halford Luccock wrote a book on sermon construction entitled *In The Minister's Workshop*. The pastor's study should be a workshop where a sermon is designed and built. Each of us needs to learn how to prepare a sermon.

Two-fold Preparation

Writing a sermon demands preparation. The most important part of preparation is spiritual. Before sermon construction begins, time must be spent in prayer, Bible reading, meditation, solitude and reflection. This creates a spiritual mood, and only "spiritually-minded people can apprehend spiritual truth," as the apostle Paul said. As

Bach wrote on the first page of a composition, so a preacher would do well to write, "J.J.," "Jesu Juva"—Jesus help!

A parish pastor can become so busy with parish business that personal devotions may be neglected. After the PTL television ministry scandal, Jim Bakker's second in command, Richard Dortch, explained, "We were so caught up in God's work that we forgot about God."

Intellectual preparation for the sermon is also necessary. This involves study, writing and rewriting. Preaching calls for hours of hard work. For me, I found as a parish pastor that preaching was the hardest thing I had to do. "Preach" can be broken down to two words, "preach(e)." For many of us preparing a sermon is absolute agony, followed by ecstasy when the sermon is delivered.

There is no short and easy way to become an effective preacher. It calls for a minimum of twenty hours per week of study, preferably four hours each morning for five days.

Lack of study accounts for today's inferior preaching. For example, one pastor stays up all Saturday night to prepare his sermon because he claims he needs the time pressure to get the sermon ready. Another pastor advised a fellow-pastor, "Just turn off your television at ten Saturday night and spend the hour before you go to bed outlining your sermon. That's what I do."

My first year of ministry I was an assistant pastor. Occasionally when the choir and pastors waited in the narthex for the prelude to end and the processional hymn to begin, the senior pastor would ask me, "John, do you have a text to suggest for today?" What an example he set for the beginning of my ministry!

Some years ago William Self published a book of two hundred sermon outlines entitled *The Saturday Night Special.* The big question each minister must face is, Are you willing to settle for "Saturday night specials," or will you pay the price of being a good preacher? Are you ready to spend at least twenty hours week after week struggling, agonizing over your sermon? Good preaching calls for blood, sweat and tears.

Getting an Idea

The crux of a good sermon is a good idea. What shall I preach about? What will be the subject?

For good ideas, you must start with devotional time with God, for the Holy Spirit is the one who will give the ideas, thoughts, insights and truths to be preached.

Then, as you think of a subject for preaching, consider your local situation. What is the season of the church year? Is it a festival such as Pentecost or All Saints Sunday? Is this Sunday a national holiday: Memorial Day, Independence Day, Mother's or Father's Day? Is there anything special taking place in the local congregation—Confirmation or Communion? The choice of a subject might be geared to the occasion, season or Sunday.

Though an idea for a sermon is given by the Holy Spirit, the Spirit works through both the Word and the world. In reading the Bible, a verse or passage may strike you and call you to preach on it. Or you might review the lessons in the lectionary for a possible text. If the idea comes from the Word, it must then be related to the world that it may speak to today's human situation. On the other hand, the idea may come from the world: a book recently read, an overheard conversation, a counseling session, a movie scene, a life situation. For example, I may hear a bishop give an invocation at a national political convention without praying in the name of Christ, and the idea for a sermon comes to me: Is Christ really necessary for a good life? Can we get along just as well without him?

If the idea comes from the world, we must then go to the Word for a text that gives the answer or solution to that need. If we do not go to the Word, the sermon will become merely topical, limited to the preacher's human solution to the problem being addressed.

The Text

Once we have the idea or subject in mind, we turn to the text. The text is the most important part of a sermon because, as God's Word, it is the source of the sermon's truth.

Exegesis, the study of the text, follows. With the aid of biblical languages, Bible dictionary, concordance, word book and commentaries, we learn the truth of the text through exegesis. We look at the passage in its context. We ask what the text means for life today.

Out of this exegetical study of the text comes the basic elements upon which the sermon is built: 1) The precis of the text—a writing out of the text in our own words to show that we understand the text; 2) The thesis of the text—a one-sentence summary of the truth of the text; 3) The theme of the text—a facet of the thesis to be preached. This theme becomes the theme of the sermon. The theme is usually written out as an incomplete sentence which is completed by the main points in the outline.

The Need

Before we can proceed with sermon preparation, we must decide if the sermon is needed by the local congregation. If there is no need, there is no reason to prepare it. This calls for knowing the people in the pews. Every person has a need, and the sermon should be designed to meet that need. At his ashrams, E. Stanley Jones passed out slips of paper saying, "No one will see what you are about to write on this paper. I want you to write what your need is today." One person responded, "Brother Stanley, I don't have a need. What do you write down if you don't have a need?" Dr. Jones replied, "If you don't think you have a need, then *that's* your need."

It is not enough to design the sermon around a universal need. For example, "All people are sinners and need a Savior" is too general for a specific sermon. What is the local, specific need with which the chosen text deals? A sermon that does not answer a particular need is useless, a waste of time and energy. On a preacher's worksheet, he or she must write out the need and then compare it with the proposed text.

The Objective

The need of the sermon and its objective are closely related. The aim, objective or purpose of the sermon is to meet the need. It is essential to ask, "What do I want to accomplish with this sermon? What do I want the people to do?"

A student preacher gave his sermon to his practice preaching class and professor. After the class he went to the professor's office for the critique. The student waited in fear and trembling for the professor's criticism. The teacher was silent. The student could not wait any longer and asked, "It will do, sir, won't it? It will do?" The professor replied, "Do what?"

In general, a sermon has a three-fold aim, as taught by Cicero: "An eloquent man must speak as to teach, to delight, and to persuade." A sermon has as its goal to interest the people, enlighten their minds and stir their wills to surrender to Christ and obey his call to discipleship.

But a sermon must have a specific objective. In light of the need you established, what do you hope to accomplish? A new understanding? A different attitude? A course of action? The goal or aim is so important that along with the text and need, it should be written out at the top of the worksheet. This aim is so vital that it determines what the introduction should be. The main points of the outline are steps toward the objective, and the conclusion is an appeal to actualize the aim.

The Outline

What are you going to say about the subject related to the text? How can you say anything unless you first know what you want and need to say? An outline answers these questions. The outline has three main parts: introduction, body and conclusion.

The Introduction

Plato said, "The beginning is the most important part of the work." The introduction is not only the most important but the most difficult part of the sermon to prepare. The introduction is difficult to write because it must accomplish so much in a very short time. It must be brief, just long enough to accomplish its purpose. An introduction is meant to arouse interest, to get attention, to state the problem, need, situation or question. It must hook the congregation so that they will want to hear the rest of the message. To catch the people's interest the introduction should begin with the here and now, with people or with a pressing problem or need. It is said that if a speaker does not get his audience in the first thirty seconds, he or she does not ever involve them in the message.

The Body

The body of the sermon consists of the theme and the message's main points. How many points should a sermon have? A sermon should have only *one* point. That one point is the theme, and it is the theme of the biblical text. The theme results from the prior work of exegesis. The main points of the sermon are only sub-points of the one overall point, the theme. We have one thing to get across, one truth to proclaim. One theme is enough for a twenty-minute sermon, because of the time needed to break it down and to explain, illustrate and apply it to daily life. The number of main points under the theme is determined by the text, usually no less than two points and no more than four.

It is important how these main points are stated and in what order they appear. The main points must always be stated in connection with the theme so that the message is unified with one theme, one truth, one impact. The main points also need to be brief, simple and easy to remember. Alliteration of the points is helpful. Note the parallelism in the following outline on the Prodigal Son:

A. His madness
B. His sadness
C. His gladness

An outline also needs balance. Each main point

should be in proportion to the others lest one point overshadow the others and leave the impression that this sub-point is the main point of the sermon. In listing the main points the text needs to be considered in its own order of development.

The Conclusion

As with the introduction, the conclusion is very difficult to prepare. A common mistake is to make the conclusion a summary of the main points. If a sermon were a lecture this would be appropriate. But a sermon is more than a learning experience. A sermon calls for decision and action. It is the time for an appeal to put into practice the truth of the text. It answers the question, "What then shall we do?"

Like an introduction, the conclusion is brief. An ideal conclusion refers back to the introduction. When the introduction and conclusion are brought together it is like tying a bow on a gift package.

Because of their importance and because every word counts, the introduction and conclusion should be memorized.

Open the Drapes!

It is time to open the drapes and let the light shine on the material in the body of the sermon. In the preparation of the outline, we have a skeleton and structure for the sermon. Now we need a filler. What are we going to say about the main points? Each main point is developed by argumentation, explanation, application and illumination.

In order to illuminate a point, illustrative material is needed to throw light on the subject. We need facts, figures, similes, metaphors, stories, illustrations, personal experiences, historical events, literary references, etc. Now is the time to review the homiletical material in your storehouse, the materials you have been gathering for years. As you go through your file, notebook or drawer where you keep the illustrative material, look for items that apply to a particular point. Also, reflect on your own life to see if any personal experience could be used.

A sermon devoid of illustrations is heavy and dark. Illustrations throw light on a subject so that the hearers say, "Now I see what you mean." In addition, illustrations help a preacher to maintain the people's interest.

The Language

We have come to the point in sermon preparation that many preachers dislike and thereby neglect: writing the sermon. It is a tedious and time-consuming task. Yet for good preaching a sermon must be written down. You know what you want to say, but how will you say it—what words, what phrases? The value of writing out the sermon is not to have something to read to the people but to find fitting words and phrases to say it.

In writing the sermon, remember that you are not writing a chapter in a book, an article for a magazine or a term paper for a seminary course. A sermon is not meant to be read but to be heard. This calls for oral writing. You write for the ear rather than for the eye. You write as you would normally talk in a conversation. You are talking to people, not to pews. To help you attain this goal, imagine your congregation members seated in their accustomed pews and talk to them personally. There is the Smith family. Over here are Mary and Joe. Talk to them, eye to eye, about God.

This style of writing involves language of a special type. You are not talking to theologians or to Bible scholars. These are plain, ordinary people wanting to hear a message from God. Speak their language. Though the English dictionary has 500,000 words, the average person uses only six hundred. Use simple words to be understood. Make your sentences short, concise and declarative. Involve your listeners in the message. Refer to them; ask them questions.

It is important also to write in such a way that the skeleton of the sermon can be seen by the ear. The main points of the theme need to be clear and pronounced.

There should be a transition from one point to another. Why is this necessary? When reading, if a person does not get a point or does not understand something, he or she can turn back and read the paragraph a second time. But in a sermon this cannot be done. The sermon goes by so quickly that listeners can easily miss the point. When you write, you capitalize, underline and italicize things of importance. But how do you do this in oral communication? You make your points clear and you use good transitions which are bridges from one point to the next. You also can use repetition. Unless the structure is visible, the people may receive a mere impression from the sermon, but they will not be able to repeat what was said. This is tragic because we preach the Word, the word of truth. A feeling or impression soon dissolves but the truth is what should stay with them. Make your sermon so clear and simple that one of your listeners could repeat its main points to someone who didn't hear the sermon himself.

The Final Step

A bell is not a bell until it is rung. A song is not a song until it is sung. A sermon is not a sermon until it is preached. You have come to the final step in preaching, the delivery of the sermon. You have the sermon written out. It is on your desk. What do you do with it?

You do nothing with it! You put it in your file. You prepare to deliver it by working from your outline. Except for the introduction and conclusion, you memorize not words or sentences but ideas as listed on the outline. Silently or audibly go over the sermon as often as necessary until you feel confident with it. A long interval should come between each time you go over the message, because this helps the memory. Sleep on it, and when Sunday comes you are, with God's help, ready to deliver your soul and God's message to his people.

Inductive Preaching

In a conversation once with an avowed atheist, Harry Emerson Fosdick said to the atheist, "Tell me about the god you don't believe in. Perhaps I don't believe in him either."

In this case Fosdick used the inductive method, the same method he usually used in his preaching. If he had used the deductive approach, he might have quoted Psalm 14:1, "The fool says in his heart, 'There is no God.'" Then he might have gone on to advance the ontological, cosmological, teleological and moral arguments for the existence of God. In the end, do you think he would have won over the atheist to a belief in God?

Many people today are turned off by the deductive style of presentation whether in teaching, counseling or preaching. They are products of a scientific mindset which seeks truth through the collection of data, experimentation, classification, research and coming to their own conclusions. Today people do not want to be bulldozed into truth. They do not want to be told what to think or believe. They want to find out for themselves.

In educational circles the deductive lecture has been replaced by dialogue and discussion, with the teacher serving as a leader and guide in search of the truth. For this reason the most suitable and acceptable style of preaching for our day is the inductive rather than the deductive style. In order to understand the inductive style, we need to contrast it with the deductive method.

The Deductive Method

The deductive method of preaching is the traditional style of past generations. Its slogan is "Thus saith the Lord." It is declarative and dogmatic. The only acceptable response is to accept and obey.

A deductive sermon begins with a statement of a truth or principle. Often with the principle there is an explanation of the biblical, historical and theological source of the truth. The truth is then explained, broken down into its component parts or applied to different categories. This same procedure is used in debating. A resolution is stated, such as "Capital punishment is a sin." Two teams debate the truth or falsehood of the statement. In academic papers, a writer is expected to state the thesis of the paper and the main point of the theme. Then he or she proceeds to analyze the theme accordingly. In the conclusion the main points are summarized.

Some preachers think this should be done in sermons. A slave preacher once explained his method, "I tells them what I am going to say. I tells them, and then I tells them what I said." The same deductive method was used in a recently published sermon. The opening paragraph:

> My purpose is to present Christ to you as Matthew saw him; to share with you Christ's purpose for the world as Matthew understood it; and to encourage our response to that purpose as Matthew would have wanted it.

In this opening sentence we are given the truth and purposes of the sermon. But some could say, "I got the message. So, let's go home." From that point on, they may feel there is nothing else to be heard except an amplification of the sermon's points.

A deductive sermon goes from the general to the specific. It starts out with a statement of the truth, the answer to the question or the solution to the problem. The direction is from top to bottom. What is said is deduced from the general principle. It is illustrated by this diagram:

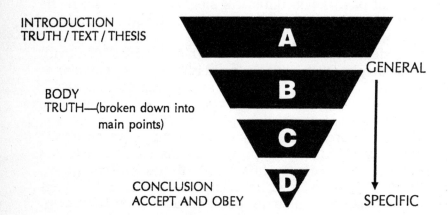

There are disadvantages and advantages to the deductive method. Consider the following:

Disadvantages:

1. It is an outmoded style of communication.

2. The authoritative method turns contemporary listeners off as being dogmatic.

3. Telling the truth, answer or solution at the start causes a loss of interest in what follows.

4. The congregation is put in a passive position; they have nothing to do but listen.

5. The preacher does your thinking for you.

Advantages:

1. Some people want an authoritative message telling them what to think, believe and do. This is an appeal of religious cults.

2. The message is characterized by certainty and conviction. There is only one way to think. This is the absolute truth. There is no doubt, confusion or uncertainty.

3. The Bible is used as the sole source of truth.

The Inductive Word

In contrast to the deductive, the inductive method begins with the specific and goes to the general. It goes from bottom to top instead of top to bottom. The slogan is, "Come, let us reason together" (Isaiah 1:18). The introduction presents the case, a problem, a question or a need. What is the answer or solution? What are the possibilities or the options? What do you think? The method can be seen in the diagram below:

What shape or structure does an inductive sermon take? Consider the usual steps:

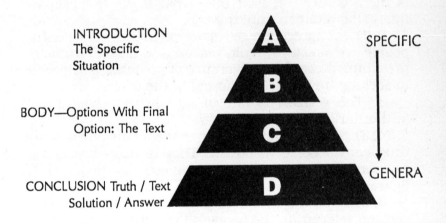

1. Introduction—begin with the here and now with a specific, concrete case, situation, problem or need.

2. Body—explore the possible options, answers or solutions. As the final option, consider the text as the answer.

3. Conclusion—appeal for the acceptance of the biblical solution according to the text.

Disadvantages:

1. There is a possible loss of authority of God's Word. One view may be considered as good as another. The voice

of God may be drowned out by the cacophony of human voices.

2. The answer or solution comes as the last option. Only one-third or one-fourth of the sermon time is given to it. This may be inadequate to explain, illustrate and apply the biblical answer.

3. The subject may be left open-ended and the people leave without a definite answer or solution to the need.

4. The text is in danger of being minimized or neglected.

Advantages:

1. Interest, curiosity and suspense are aroused. What is the answer? If it isn't this, what is it? The people's interest is retained until the end.

2. The congregation gets involved in the message. The people are asked to think, reason and decide. It makes preaching a cooperative venture of preacher and people in seeking the truth to be found in the text.

3. The sermon is one of authority without being authoritarian or dogmatic.

4. The people come to their own conclusions and are thus convinced of the truth. They develop a personal conviction rather than a belief imposed by an authority figure.

5. The specific situation, problem or need makes the sermon relevant to the people's lives. The sermon deals with people where they are and what they are facing in life.

Exhibits of the Inductive Method

Jesus

In his teaching and preaching Jesus used the inductive method. He usually let the people discover the truth for themselves. He never said dogmatically, "I am the Christ" or "I am the Son of God." He let the people discover that and come to their own conclusion about who he was. In answering questions he asked questions. He presented a situation for the people's consideration. He told stories (parables) as a way of presenting truth in an indirect way. He used specifics: sheep, seed, lamp, child, coin, etc. He took advantage of immediate situations: a woman caught in adultery, a dinner in a friend's home, his feet being washed by a prostitute, people choosing the chief seats at a banquet, etc.

Peter

The first Christian sermon delivered on Pentecost (Acts 2:14-36) was an inductive sermon.

A. Peter begins with the current situation: drunkenness (v. 15)

B. Peter quotes passages familiar to the people (vv. 17-21)

C. Peter refers to the people's experience (vv. 22-23)

D. Peter concludes: "This Jesus" (v. 32)

Paul

Paul preaches to the intelligentsia in Athens (Acts 17:21-31).

A. He establishes rapport with the Greeks: "Very religious" (v. 22)

B. He refers to the local situation: "altars" (v. 23)

C. He quotes their own authors, not the Bible (v. 28)

D. He addresses their concern: "new" (v. 21)

E. He concludes with an appeal (v. 30)

A Contemporary Possibility

The situation: Someone says to a group of children, "God's greatest gift to you is your life. You must take care of it."

A. Begin with the question: What is God's greatest gift to you?

B. Consider the options:

1. Is God's greatest gift life? Is this the answer? What is life without Christ?

2. Is it love? What is love without Christ?

3. Is it truth? What is truth apart from Christ?

4. Is it Christ? Consider the text: John 3:16.

A Wedding of the Two Approaches

Shall I be a deductive or an inductive preacher? Must it be one or the other? Why not both? The ideal is to be deductive in the content in order to make certain that the Word is heard and to be inductive in order for the message to be accepted by contemporary hearers.

By the way, have you noticed that this chapter was written according to the inductive method?

Chapter 23

Dialogical Preaching

When you preach, are you speaking to the pews or to the people? Are you talking to, at or with God's people? Your answer to the questions reveals whether or not you are a dialogical preacher.

Dialogical preaching is not dialogue preaching. The latter is performed by two or more speakers, lay or clerical, in a back-and-forth conversation about a text, with the congregation "overhearing" your discussion. Dialogical preaching is done by one person who is speaking with a congregation about a text.

Although dialogical preaching is a new emphasis in preaching, it is really nothing new. The Old Testament prophets used this method of communication. Malachi uses the question-and-answer technique of dialogue: "Will a man rob God? Yet you rob me. But you ask, 'How do we rob you?' In tithes and offerings" (Malachi 3:8). In Ezekiel, Yahweh says, "Yet the house of Israel says, 'The way of the Lord is not just.' Are my ways unjust, O house of Israel?" (Ezekiel 18:29).

John the Baptizer was a dialogical preacher. He senses what his congregation is saying: "And do not think you can say to yourselves, 'We have Abraham as our father.' I tell you that out of these stones God can raise up children for Abraham" (Matthew 3:9).

Jesus also was a master of dialogical teaching and preaching. At Caesarea Philippi, Jesus knew the time had come for the disciples to realize that he was the Messiah.

But he did not make a declarative and authoritative claim. He did not try to persuade the men that he was the Christ. He used the dialogical method of questioning: "Who do men say that the Son of man is?" and "Who do you say that I am?"

Repeatedly Jesus answered a question by asking a question. At times he allowed the people to decide: "Which is easier: to say, 'Your sins are forgiven,' or to say, 'Get up and walk'" (Matthew 9:5)? Once Jesus asked a lawyer to make up his own mind about the meaning of a teaching. At the close of the Good Samaritan parable he asked, "Which of these three *do you think* was a neighbor to the man who fell into the hands of robbers?" (Luke 10:36, italics mine).

Dialogical preaching is a change from traditional sermons, which are usually monological, formal and almost dictatorial. The listeners are expected to be passive, taking it all in and obeying. But times have changed and most people today do not appreciate this "bellowing forth" from a "holy pedestal." Today people want to hear a message of authority without it being given in an authoritarian manner. They want to see a real person in the pulpit who speaks *with* them about God's Word.

One problem with dialogical preaching is that it is often given in a casual, low voice. One gets the impression that the preacher is not deeply concerned about what he or she is saying. The impression given is "You can take it or leave it." However, dialogical preaching can and should be done with vitality and animation. A dialogical preacher can speak with conviction and enthusiasm.

How to Become Dialogical

Dialogical preaching is possible only by making the appropriate approach. As the preacher you should not take the position of "knowing it all" and thinking that you alone have the whole truth. Indeed, you do have the truth of God's Word, for you spent at least twenty hours of research and thinking on the text. Yet you do not want to take an authoritarian stance, because people will resist you. Rather, you want to say with Isaiah, "'Come now, let us reason together,' says the Lord" (Isaiah 1:18). With Jesus you ask, "What do you think?" With this non-authoritarian approach, people will listen, think and get involved in the subject of the sermon.

Consider yourself in conversation with each person in the congregation. This will eliminate an oratorical and pompous style to which contemporary audiences will not respond. The person in the pulpit must come across as a real human being. The tone of his or her voice must be natural. Gestures must come automatically and spontaneously rather than being studied and improvised. Dialogical preaching is animated conversation filled with enthusiasm and joy.

Involve the congregation in the sermon. Refer often to the people as "you," not "they." "We" is fine for including the preacher in what is said. Ask questions: "Have you had the experience . . . ?" or "Did you see in yesterday's paper . . . ?" or "You may be asking yourself . . . ?" Anticipate the people's questions and thinking. To be able to do this, it is necessary to know your people intimately: What are they saying, what are they thinking, how are they reacting to what is being said?

When a preacher deals with everyday problems, temptations, perplexities and concerns of life, the congregation says, "Hey, he's talking about me!" To be able to know one's congregation intimately, preachers must live with the people, visit in their homes, read the newspapers and magazines they read, see popular movies, read best-sellers and keep their ears to the ground throughout the week to listen to the cries and joys of the people. Then on Sundays the preacher will speak about what is really happening in the average person's life.

Speak the people's language. Avoid big words. Avoid ecclesiastical jargon. Translate theological terms like "justification" and "atonement" into words the people understand. Preach such simple phrases that anyone could know what you are talking about. Sentences need to be short and simple.

Take a cue from top communicators such as broadcaster Paul Harvey. Whenever he frets that a script for a radio broadcast might be too esoteric or too boring, he administers the "Aunt Betty" test. He re-reads the story with his sister-in-law in mind. She likes her news sometimes sweet, sometimes spicy, but always the kind that slides down easily. He won't use fifty-cent words on Betty. He explains, "If Betty can't understand it, or if it wouldn't catch her interest, or if it dwells too much on technicalities, I throw it away and start over."

Eye contact while preaching is very important. If you are speaking to a person, do you avoid looking him in the eye? Take a tip from television: note how speakers, news reporters and commentators look directly into the camera in order to seem like they are directly communicating with viewers. When you preach, are your eyes on the ceiling, the windows or your notes? Maybe you project a non-committal stare at the congregation without really seeing anybody. Or maybe you close your eyes while speaking! When we talk with anyone, an individual or a group of people, we must keep our eyes on the hearers just as we want them to look at us while we preach. To maintain constant eye contact, we must know the sermon so well that constant reference to notes is not necessary. People then feel that you are speaking not only from the mind but from the heart as well. They feel that you are really talking to them. (See chapter twenty-four for more on eye contact.)

Don't you want to become a dialogical preacher? Well, respond! Do you or don't you? In dialogical fashion, I have spoken to you. Now it is time for you to respond!

The Visual Element in Preaching

There is much more to a sermon than speaking and hearing words. Much stress should be placed upon proper enunciation, pronunciation, phrasing and speed of speech. Almost every congregation now has a public address system to be sure that the sermon is heard, and some congregations make special provisions for hearing-impaired people by installing amplification devices in the pews.

But a sermon is more than words. A sermon is seen as well as heard. It is an event, a happening before the congregation's eyes. In writing to the Thessalonian church, the apostle Paul reminds the people that his preaching was more than words: "Our gospel came to you not simply with words but also with power, with the Holy Spirit and with deep conviction" (1 Thessalonians 1:5).

Non-verbal Communication

A sermon is a communication event which involves both preacher and people, both ear and eye. This communication is verbal and non-verbal. Of the two, the non-verbal is more effective in getting a message across and making sure it is received. In an article, *Communication without Words*, Albert Meharbian reports the results of a study dealing with communication. According to this study, seven percent of a message comes through words, thirty-eight percent through tone of voice and fifty-five percent comes through body language. He maintains that a person's non-verbal behavior generally has more bearing on communicating feelings and attitudes than do words.

According to these figures, less than one-third of communication takes place through spoken language. Body language includes all physical movements: use of eyes, facial expressions, posture, movements and mannerisms. Body language can add to or detract from the communication process. It is possible for the preacher to be saying one thing with his or her voice and the opposite with his or her body, thus canceling out the message.

To get the maximum benefit from non-verbal communication, both preacher and people need to be visible to each other. The preacher needs to be seen while preaching. The pulpit needs to be elevated so that worshipers in the back pews can see him or her.

The elevated pulpit does not signify that the preacher is on a higher plane than the people, and it does not mean that the preacher is an authoritarian figure speaking down to the people. The elevated pulpit simply enables everyone to see the preacher. Spotlights on the pulpit aid the audience in seeing the speaker.

However, care must be taken that the spotlight is not directly over the preacher's head, for this will cause shadows to fall on his or her eyes, thus hindering preacher/congregation eye contact. Nor should a spotlight be placed directly in front of the pulpit lest it be too bright for the preacher and he or she will not be able to see the people. The most effective place for spotlights is to have one on each side of the nave. This enables both sides of the preacher's face to be seen.

The preacher also needs to see the congregation, for preaching is a two-way communication. The people communicate with the preacher while the sermon is in progress. Their communication can be both verbal and non-verbal. The verbal may be an "Amen" or "Preach on!"

or "Praise the Lord." The non-verbal consists of the people's physical responses. They may nod their heads in agreement or shake their heads to communicate disagreement.

For the preacher to see the people while preaching, a proper seating arrangement is necessary. A church in the round makes it difficult for the pastor to see all of the people. No matter which way the preacher turns he or she can see only one-fourth of the congregation. A church in St. Petersburg, Florida, tries to overcome this problem by having a rotating chancel and pulpit.

For a preacher to see the people, the nave needs to be properly illuminated during the sermon. As the sermon begins, the pulpit spotlight should be turned on and the lights in the nave dimmed. The darkened church helps the people to relax and to be receptive to the message. However, it is possible that the nave can be too dark for the preacher to see the people's faces. It is good to lower the lights during the sermon, but not to the point where the preacher must speak into a dark void. If this happens a preacher is prevented from seeing the people's reactions to the sermon.

Eye Contact

The most effective aspect of non-verbal communication is eye contact. This involves the use or non-use of a manuscript or notes. If a manuscript is read, naturally the preacher's eyes are on the paper. If notes are used, the sermon's effectiveness decreases according to how often the preacher refers to the notes. Eye contact is like a laser beam of communication between pulpit and pew. Each time the eye is taken off the speaker or hearer, the line of communication is broken. If a reference to notes breaks the person-to-person line, it must be restored before communication can continue. Obviously, then, the most effective form of preaching is constant eye contact, referring to notes as little as possible.

Why do we claim that preaching without notes is the

most effective type of sermon communication? Think of the advantages:

Communication. By eye contact the people see the truth as well as hear it. The people see what you mean. The sermon becomes more convincing and moving.

Feedback. When the preacher has his or her eyes on the people, he or she receives their messages by visual means. The people are telling the preacher something about the message. The preacher sees whether they are bored and disinterested, or caught up in the message. Are they reading the church bulletin, looking out the window or whispering to a neighbor? Negative feedback helps a preacher analyze this communication and improve sermon delivery. Good feedback encourages and inspires the preacher to do even better. With a constant eye on the congregation, the preacher can make adjustments and adaptations according to the moment.

Directness. How do you feel when the person to whom you are speaking looks away from you? Do you not get the impression that he or she is really interested in something else? When a congregation hears a preacher who does not look at them, they get the impression that the message is not for them. Look at a person—eye to eye—and you are saying, "I mean you. I am talking to you!"

A mother took her young son to hear the great preacher Charles H. Spurgeon. As Spurgeon spoke, the lad tugged on his mother's sleeve and asked, "Mother, is Mr. Spurgeon speaking to me?"

Dialogue. If a sermon is a two-way communication process, eye contact enables a dialogical message. People and preacher are in conversation with each other. He or she is aware of their presence, speaks to them, asks them questions and expects their responses. This dialogue would be impossible without eye contact.

Freedom. Getting away from notes gives freedom to the preacher. He or she is not imprisoned behind a paper curtain and can adapt to unusual conditions in the congregation and utilize them to get the message across.

CHAPTER 24 **■** 173

He or she can modify the message as feedback comes to the pulpit. There is freedom to move about in the pulpit or even to come out of the pulpit to make a point because the preacher is not chained to a manuscript.

Of course, there are some disadvantages. Every practice can be abused. Preaching without notes can indicate little or no preparation or suggest impromptu speaking. Sometimes the sermon gets too wordy and lengthy. It is possible to become repetitious and to take thought detours. It might be possible to use a better choice of words and phrasing.

A preacher who doesn't use notes constantly tries to avoid these disadvantages.

How to Preach Without Notes

If the non-use of notes is so effective in communicating the Word, is it possible for everyone to adopt the method as a regular practice? It does not take a genius to do it, only hard labor. Writing out a sermon and then reading it is the easiest way to deliver it. Preaching without notes requires extra labor and time. It is probably for this reason that few preach without notes. So, how does one learn to preach without notes?

1. Begin your sermon preparation at least a week in advance to give your subject time to soak in. Saturate yourself with the subject until it becomes second nature to you.

2. Draw up a simple, coherent outline. The simpler the outline, the easier it will be to preach without notes.

3. Write out the sermon so you can find the proper words and phrases to express your ideas. Then put the manuscript aside and work only with your outline.

4. Memorize your outline in terms of ideas rather than words or sentences.

5. Go over the sermon word for word in your mind approximately three times. Let several hours go by before going through the sermon again. If possible, sleep on the sermon to allow your subconscious mind to work.

6. After your diligent preparation, throw yourself on

the mercy of God in complete trust and dependence on the Holy Spirit to use you mightily.

7. During the sermon you may wish to keep a general outline in front of you to glance at if your mind goes blank.

and hearts open to the Spirit who speaks through the Word?

John R. W. Stott offered this prayer which could serve as a model: "Heavenly Father, we bow in your presence. May your Word be our rule, your Spirit our teacher, and your greater glory our supreme concern."

As a parish pastor for a number of years, I had my congregation form the habit of praying for the preacher and for their receptivity immediately before the sermon. While the organist softly played one more stanza of the hymn before the sermon, the people united in silent prayer which concluded with my pulpit prayer. In this way, we prayed for each other before the proclamation of the Word.

This practice runs counter to some contemporary orders of worship that have the sermon immediately following the gospel lesson and the hymn of the day coming after the sermon. In my opinion this is a mistake. Both preacher and people need a transition time from the three lessons to the sermon. The hymn before the sermon prepares the people for the theme of the sermon and gives the preacher time to collect his or her thoughts for preaching without notes.

Sentence Prayer

The pulpit prayer should be a sentence prayer. A longer prayer detracts from the pastoral and general prayer that often follows the sermon. But because this prayer is confined to a sentence, it requires much preparation. Each word in the sentence should have meaning.

Consider this, for example: "Grant, dear Father, that what we hear with our ears we may believe in our hearts, and what we believe in our hearts we may practice in our lives."

The sentence prayer should relate to the theme of the sermon. Along with the hymn it helps the congregation begin thinking about the truth of that day's sermon. Thus, for an effective sentence prayer you must know your aim, goal or purpose for your sermon. What do you want your people to do or think as a result of your sermon? The sentence prayer deals with that sermon idea.

Also, each sermon needs its own sentence prayer to avoid repetitiveness, for if the same prayer is used Sunday after Sunday, people tend not to hear it after a while and its effectiveness is lost.

Sample Prayers

There are many resources for the prayer before the sermon. You may want to use a contemporary reference to arouse interest in the sermon. Consider this: "Dear God, if it is true that the world listens when E. F. Hutton speaks, how much more should we listen when you speak to us through your Word?"

A hymn may suggest a prayer:

> O fill us with thy fullness, Lord,
> Until our very hearts o'erflow
> In kindling thought and glowing word
> Thy love to tell, Thy praise to show.

Psalms may suggest a pulpit prayer:

> "Show [us] your ways, O Lord, teach [us] your paths; guide [us] in your truth and teach [us]" (Psalm 25:4,5).

> "Send forth your light and your truth, let them guide [us]; let them bring [us] to your holy mountain, to the place where you dwell" (Psalm 43:3).

> "Your word is a lamp to [our] feet and a light for [our] path" (Psalm 119:105).

Preaching is an awesome experience! How can a preacher and congregation enter into it without an appeal to God for help both to declare and to receive the precious, life-giving Word?

Chapter 26

What Happens After the Sermon?

What happens after the sermon? Should there be a response by the people? Many churches place the sermon as the last item in the order of worship. At the end of most sermons a hymn is sung and the benediction is pronounced. In this type of service, there is no opportunity for worshipers to react to the sermon. Does the preacher expect a response? If so, what kind of response is desired? Does the order of worship make provision for a response?

The issue comes down to what a sermon should accomplish. Is it meant to entertain or to educate? Then there is little need for congregational response. At the end of the sermon, do you say, "Have a good day, folks!" or "Enjoy your Sunday dinner!"? But if a sermon is to move people to action, to a resolution or to a decision, then it is essential that people are given an opportunity to respond.

In speaking of a response to the sermon, we are not thinking about a response during the sermon in terms of "Amen" or "Praise the Lord." A story is told of a Methodist who visited a Lutheran worship service. The pastor preached with enthusiasm and conviction. The Methodist was moved to loudly say, "Amen!" A little later he called out, "Hallelujah!" Members of the congregation were disturbed. Finally an usher came up to him and whispered, "Sir, you have to behave yourself or you'll have to leave." The visitor replied, "I can't help it, sir. I've got religion." The usher whispered back, "Well, you didn't get it here. So keep quiet."

A Response

What response do we want from the people between the sermon and the benediction? A good sermon voices a call to follow Jesus. A true sermon throws down a challenge to the people to believe, to love, to confess their sins, to repent, to surrender to Christ or to serve. The sermon is a call to action, to a resolution and to a decision. We preach in the hope that a life will be changed, a person will be transformed and a new road will be taken.

If we preach and plead and urge and call for such action, should we deprive people of the opportunity to express their new-found faith and love of God? When God calls, he expects an answer. Without allowing for response, the sermon may be only an emotional spree, an entertaining presentation or an intelligent exercise. But a biblical sermon must have as its ultimate objective to persuade, to convince the mind and to stir the will to action. If a response from the people is not allowed the sermon itself is in vain.

This contention that there should be a response to the sermon is biblically valid. A response is always expected when the Word is proclaimed. When Jonah preached to Nineveh, the reaction was great: "The Ninevites believed God. They declared a fast, and all of them, from the greatest to the least, put on sackcloth" (Jonah 3:5). Again, at the close of a sermon by John the Baptist the people asked him, "What should we do then?" (Luke 3:10). After the first Christian sermon at Pentecost, the people were so moved that they asked the apostles, "Brothers, what shall we do?" (Acts 2:37). Even today when the gospel is forcefully preached and God's claims are presented, people in the pews silently ask the preacher, "What shall we do about it?" Tragically, the preacher often does not hear their question.

An Appropriate Response

Not every kind of response to a sermon is appropriate. At least two principles should be kept in mind. One is that the response to the sermon should be corporate. Every person in the service needs to respond to God's Word. Every person, including faithful church members, is a sinner in need of repentance. Every person in the church needs to believe in God more deeply, to love Christ more and to follow more closely the guidance of the Spirit.

Some churches today follow the sermon with an "altar call" or an "opening the doors of the church" for membership. During the singing of the last hymn, the congregation waits for one or two "sinners" to confess Christ or for visitors to come forward to join the church.

Unfortunately, these decisions apply only to about one percent of the congregation. Ninety-nine percent of the audience is given no opportunity to respond, because they already are Christians and/or church members. The unchurched are no longer in worship services waiting to be evangelized. Today the church generally seeks and gains new converts and members through personal evangelism, lay visitation and preparatory education for church membership. Using the Sunday sermon regularly for evangelism is ineffective in today's world.

The second principle of a response is variety. One invitation to respond does not meet the needs of all people. People have different needs and react differently to sermons. Walking down an aisle and shaking hands with the preacher may be satisfactory for some but not for all. There are many ways to provide opportunity for worshipers to respond to the Word.

Congregational Response

We have seen that the preacher must make some provision in the order of service for a congregational response. Liturgical churches have a built-in response in the liturgy. The sermon comes about midway through the service and is followed by several opportunities for a response to the Word which has been read and proclaimed.

After the sermon, the congregation may confess a creed as a response of faith: "I believe in God. . . ." The offering is received after the sermon as a response to God's gifts. The offering consists of our love gifts offered as an act of worship. The members of the congregation also have an opportunity to rededicate themselves by participating in the offertory, which is usually a canticle based on a psalm. A further response is provided in the offering of our prayers, our petitions and expressions of thanksgiving and praise for God's goodness. These opportunities come after the sermon as responses to God's Word.

Non-liturgical churches are realizing their need of a response to the sermon other than the traditional altar call. After the sermon an offering can be received as an act of response to God's providence. The pastoral prayer may follow the sermon. As a means of corporate rededication and commitment, a hymn of discipleship may be used. When the sermon is concluded there can be a period of silence for reflection on the message. Occasionally cards can be distributed to worshipers as they enter. On these cards people may write the resolution, decision or change they intend to make in their lives. A growing practice is "altar prayers" when after the sermon, people may kneel at a communion rail for prayer while the organ plays softly.

Of course, this whole idea of responding to the sermon depends on the quality of the sermon. To make provision for a response assumes that the sermon will be moving, will stir people to action and will challenge people to a closer walk with God. Perhaps the problem of no congregational response is not only the lack of provision for a response but also the problem of the sermon. Is the sermon designed to move people to action?

Chapter 27

How Long Is Too Long?

In the middle of a sermon a man stood up to leave. The pastor asked, "Why are you leaving?" The man explained, "I am going to get a haircut." "Well," said the preacher, "why didn't you get it before you came?" The man replied, "Because I didn't need it then."

There was a time when people tolerated long sermons. John Wesley preached for three hours; Jonathan Edwards for two hours. One-hour sermons were customary in the Victorian period. But the world has changed and church people have changed too.

Today the trend is toward brief sermons. Some people say that a sermon should be no longer than eight to ten minutes. These short messages are often called homilies rather than sermons. But are we today serving people hors d'oeuvres rather than a meal? Or an appetizer instead of an entree? Robert Young's book, *Be Brief About It*, is evidence of this trend toward short sermons. Is this good or bad for the church?

Perhaps the desire for brief sermons is a symptom of the condition of today's preaching. Sermons can be so dull, boring and irrelevant that people want short sermons to reduce their misery. A pastor of a large church in Los Angeles tells of going to church early one Sunday morning. He went to the front of the building and saw a woman about to climb the front steps. Since she was old and infirm, he offered to help her. When they got to the top step she asked, "Do you know who is preaching today?" He gave her his name. Then she said, "Would you mind helping me back down the steps?"

A Relative Matter

The length of a sermon is relative. A long sermon can seem short and a short sermon can seem long. An hour with your sweetheart can seem like ten minutes or less and ten minutes in a dentist's chair can seem like an hour. The length of a sermon is not a matter of minutes or quantity of time, but of such quality that a twenty-minute sermon can seem to be only ten minutes. Henry Ward Beecher said, "The way to shorten a sermon is to make it more interesting." When people's attention is held and they are caught up in the sermon with a vital subject affecting their lives, they are not aware of the passage of time.

Of course, not all sermons can be twenty or more minutes long. The nature of the worship service determines the amount of time the sermon may have. The sermon may need to be reduced to a meditation for occasions such as funerals, weddings, Holy Communion and noon services for business people. Today's trend for weekly Communion is threatening the traditional length of the sermon because the administration of Communion as well as increased liturgy consume more time. Since most people want a morning service to be over in an hour, something must be cut to keep it within the hour. The concern of this chapter is the length of the sermon in a regular morning worship service.

Unnecessary Length

This chapter is not an argument for unnecessarily lengthy sermons, to have length just to fill up the hour of worship. For example, there is no need for lengthy sermon introductions which often consume one-third to one-half of the entire sermon. Illustrations often are stretched out so much that they overshadow the point they were meant to illustrate. The conclusions of sermons should not drip endlessly until there is not a drop of sermonic water left.

Or preachers tend to use two words when one would do. We are subject to wordiness and repetition. Often materials in our sermons are irrelevant to the main point. Sermons may be too long because the chosen subject is too broad and deep for adequate handling in one sermon; perhaps it should be spread over a series of sermons. Or sermons may be unnecessarily long because of our slow pace of delivery.

But people today are willing to listen to full-length sermons if they are interesting, helpful and relevant to their lives. The average American has time for television— six to seven hours daily. Athletic contests and movies run for hours. A concert or stage play consumes an evening. Best-selling books are voluminous. Length is not a problem if the material is captivating. Why not make a twenty-minute sermon feel like ten?

Full-length Sermons

One argument for a twenty-minute sermon is the need for religious instruction and spiritual stimulation for our congregation. The one-hour church service may be the only exposure many people have to spiritual concerns. Is one in 168 hours too much to spend in fellowship with the sacred? In a world where people are bombarded every waking hour with commercial advertising and secular appeals, they need at least one hour of instruction and inspiration in spiritual matters. An abbreviated sermon of only a few minutes cannot fill this desperate need of spiritual development.

If a sermon deals with a great text and a crucial subject, the adequate development of the subject demands more than eight minutes. It takes time to expound, illustrate and apply the text to contemporary life. A study of brief sermons shows that the subject is hardly penetrated before it ends. The problem may be described and analyzed, but there is no time for solutions or answers. What good then does the sermon do?

And if a ten-minute sermon is supposed to improve the sermon, why then would not a five-minute sermon be twice as effective? Just as length is no criterion for a good sermon, so brevity is no guarantee of helpful messages. Short sermons can be dull too. Frank Rhodes, president of Cornell University, said, "The chief function of the commencement speaker is to be brief." Lord Canning was once asked by a preacher how he enjoyed the sermon. Canning replied, "You were brief." "Ah," said the preacher, "I always like to avoid being tedious." Canning replied, "You were also tedious."

The goal of a preacher should well be making a twenty-minute sermon feel like only ten minutes. The need of our day is not for shorter but for better sermons. In a world hungry for the Bread of Life, preachers have an opportunity to serve full spiritual meals and not mere crumbs.

Chapter 28

How to Become a Better Preacher

Do you consider yourself a good preacher? If you are like most, you would say you are better than good. In his book, *Quest for Better Preaching*, Edward Markquart tells of a survey he took of pastors. Few, he reports, rated themselves "excellent" or "fair." None considered himself to be "poor." The highest number considered themselves "very good." Maybe we think we are good preachers because we are always preaching and do not get to hear other preachers who may be better. Or maybe we take too seriously the people's compliments after the service.

According to the laity, we may not be as good as we think we are. Paul's hearers said, "His speaking amounts to nothing" (2 Corinthians 10:10). Garrison Keillor said, "My problem with ministers is that I can hardly bear their sermons." In 1985 a survey was made of 782 Lutherans who dropped out of church and were asked the reason for doing so. Forty-two percent said they became inactive because of "irrelevant sermons."

After a morning service a parishioner said to the pastor as she was greeted at the front door of the church, "Oh Pastor, you'll never know what your sermon this morning meant to me." Elated, the pastor replied, "Thank you." "Oh yes," she gushed. "It was like giving a drink to a drowning man." In the light of these remarks and facts, maybe we are thinking more highly of ourselves as preachers than we ought to think.

Concern for Improvement

If we are concerned about improving our preaching, we are in good company. Even the very best have felt inadequate in preaching. Moses told Yahweh, "I am slow of speech and tongue" (Exodus 4:10). Jeremiah lamented, "I do not know how to speak" (Jeremiah 1:6). Paul admitted, "I am unskilled in preaching" (2 Corinthians 10:10, author's paraphrase).

Are preachers born or made? The answer is—probably both. Preachers are born with certain talents and qualifications that lend themselves to rhetoric and eloquence, but for the most part preachers are made. However, they are not made overnight. A preacher is forever on the way to becoming a good preacher. Each sermon is a learning experience, a rehearsal for a better one coming up next Sunday.

How are good preachers made better? Let's assume that you are a good preacher but you want to be a better one. Let's first look at some ways you will not necessarily be made a better preacher.

You will not necessarily become a better preacher only by buying and reading one of the many newly-published books on homiletics—though it is a good practice to read at least one book on preaching annually to help you keep in mind the principles of preaching.

Also, you will not be made a better preacher only by taking a continuing education course on preaching. These courses, depending on the subject and the teacher, can be helpful but they are no guarantee. Just learning methods and principles of preaching is not enough!

Nor do I believe you will become a better preacher by borrowing materials or ideas from other preachers. Using other people's sermons will not help your preaching. Workbooks and magazines of illustrations can be suggestive and helpful, but they will not make you a better preacher. Each preacher must become better through hard work.

This Is How!

How then, can a preacher become a better preacher? My suggestions are basic, but as we work on them, our sermons are sure to improve.

Know God

Our preaching will improve as our relationship with God improves. Preaching comes out of the Holy Spirit, prayer and knowledge of God. To develop this knowledge and relationship, one hour—preferably the first hour of the day—should be given to personal devotions: Bible reading, prayer and enrichment reading. This is an opportunity for reading, reflecting and being still before God.

Know the Word

To know the Bible calls for regular and faithful hours in the study of the Bible. Some pastors do not realize that a major part of their calling is to study the Word in preparation for teaching and preaching. A pastor is the congregation's theologian-in-residence. This kind of concentrated study calls for regular hours on a day-to-day basis. It provides time for reading and research. During this time a preacher learns what are the real issues of life. Then his sermons will deal with life's real problems, and the content of the sermons will be vital. It is said that the late Bishop Arthur J. Moore's wife each morning gave her husband a bottle of milk, locked the door of his study and did not let him out until noon!

Know the World

Success in preaching largely depends upon making the Word relevant to the world. Get out and into the world without becoming a part of the world. Learn what people are saying, what they are asking and what needs they have. What do they want in life? What is troubling them?

Listen to their language and on Sundays speak in their words and with their expressions.

Know the Craft

The sermon is something constructed. One must learn how to build a sermon so that the message will be communicated and accepted. Techniques are important and by practice they are perfected. A preacher can do his or her own evaluation. After each sermon, write a few notes about what you think could be improved. Then try to correct the mistakes in the next sermon. The laity will help you to know if and how well the sermon was received. A talk-back session with a small, select group of lay people might enable you to know the reaction of the congregation.

You may or may not be a good preacher. But God called you to preach, did he not? Whether you are a poor or a good preacher, God wants you to be a better preacher!

Tests of a Good Sermon

1. Is the sermon biblically-based and Christ-centered?

2. Does the sermon relate to the congregation by fulfilling a need?

3. Is the text properly understood and used?

4. Does the sermon have a clear, practical purpose?

5. Is the sermon interesting from start to finish?

6. Is the structure of the sermon plainly evident?

7. Is the sermon rationally respectable?

8. Is the sermon adequately illustrated?

9. Is the theology of the sermon evangelical?

10. Does the sermon convince one to believe, to obey and to serve?

A Self-Service Sermon Evaluation

For growth in preaching ability, evaluate your Sunday sermon on Monday and make plans for an improved sermon next Sunday.

Yes No Somewhat

1. The text and the sermon were in harmony.
2. The sermon met a need of the people.
3. The subject was timely.
4. The introduction aroused interest.
5. The theme and main points stood out.
6. The illustrative material was adequate.
7. Interest was maintained to the end.
8. The sermon involved the people.
9. The conclusion called for a decision.
10. The delivery was direct and animated.
11. The people's response was enthusiastic.

Changes and improvements to be made in the next sermon: